# Professional Learning
# Communities

## Using Data in Decision Making to Improve Student Learning

**Author**
Patrick Baccellieri, Ed.D.
Foreword by Richard F. Elmore, Ed.D.

 SHELL EDUCATION

# Professional Learning Communities
## Using Data in Decision Making to Improve Student Learning

**Editors**
Joan Irwin, M.A.
Conni Medina, M.A.Ed.

**Copy Editor**
LeAnne Bagnall

**Editorial Director**
Lori Kamola, M.S.Ed.

**Editor-in-Chief**
Sharon Coan, M.S.Ed.

**Editorial Manager**
Gisela Lee, M.A.

**Creative Director/Cover Design**
Lee Aucoin

**Print Production Manager**
Don Tran

**Interior Layout Designer**
Robin Erickson

**Publisher**
Corinne Burton, M.A.Ed.

Permission has been granted by The Board of Education of the City of Chicago to use the name South Loop Elementary School in this book.

## Shell Education
5301 Oceanus Drive
Huntington Beach, CA 92649-1030
http://www.shelleducation.com
ISBN 978-1-4258-0518-0
© 2010 Shell Education
Made in U.S.A.

# Table of Contents

The terms "profession" and "professionalism" are used quite loosely in education, often with a defensive tone. Educators would generally like to be treated "more professionally," which usually means with more deference and respect from policymakers, parents, and social critics. Real professions do not ask for respect. They claim it. Professions are defined by the ways in which they organize themselves and by the orientation they take toward the production and utilization of knowledge and practice. Professions are defined by the body of knowledge they claim as a basis for their expertise, by their participation in the creation of that body of knowledge, by the ways they organize themselves to develop, purvey, and sustain that knowledge, and (yes) by the use of that knowledge to restrict entry by nonprofessionals to their practice. Most importantly, professions have traditions of *clinical practice*, protocols and processes by which they induct members into professional practice and by which they develop and sustain the knowledge that defines their professionalism. Knowledge in professions is a *collective good*, not an attribute of individuals. I have said in other places that, by these standards, education is not a profession, but an occupation trying to become a profession, without a practice.

Patrick Baccellieri has written a book about one school's history of improvement and renewal. It is also a book about what would have to happen if education were ever to become a profession. It is a book not only about the process of school improvement, but also about the ways in which practitioners learn to take control of the knowledge that defines their practice and use it for collective ends. It is significant in many ways, not the least of which is that Patrick is writing about his own experience leading a school, and he is writing about his understanding of the experience of the practitioners in that school during the time he was its principal. In this sense, it is a book about *clinical practice*, representing that tradition in the professional literature where professionals consolidate, reflect upon, analyze, and report their experience as practitioners. In my life as an academic, I have fought, often unsuccessfully, to establish the legitimacy of this kind of literature in an academic culture that is so deeply colonized by traditional positivist epistemology that it looks with skepticism on the capacity of professionals to reflect with meaning on their own work. Mature professions allow for many forms of professional learning and discourse. It is a sign of education's insecurity that it struggles with the legitimacy of this genre. I have the deepest respect for Patrick and his academic advisors for sustaining this work.

So this is a book about the creation of a professional community written by a professional using reflection and analysis disciplined by hard evidence. In this sense, it is a model of what a profession would look like if it were ever to happen in education. There are several important themes in this analysis. One is the creation of an organizational setting in which it is safe for children and adults to learn. This is no trivial matter in an educational culture where adults often barricade themselves in their classrooms and children are shuttled from one destination to another in straight lines. Another theme is the development of organizational structures and routines where adults can actually talk to each other about common issues in their practice. A third theme is the introduction of protocols that discipline discussions of practice with evidence of its impact on the learning of children. A fourth theme is the introduction of norms of transparency of practice, in which it is okay for professionals to actually observe each other practice and to learn how to talk about their practice in ways that don't activate defensive responses. And a final theme is the development of collective efficacy and control over the use of information and the introduction of new forms of learning and knowledge to the organization. Notice the movement here, over time, from an atomized organization in which practitioners do what they know how to do, to an integrated organization in which practitioners decide what they need to know in order to do what they need to do and have the means to learn it over time. The cosmic irony of American educational reform is that it takes "reform" for schools to become places where people—adults and children—learn. As if schools had any other purpose.

Professions need strong knowledge rooted in clinical practice to grow and develop. This knowledge does not fall out of the sky into the laps of people who work in schools. Nor does it necessarily follow from academic research, no matter how well that research conforms to the established canons of academe. Professionals work at the intersection of clinical practice, organizational systems, and knowledge. If they are not engaged in actively exploiting this intersection and actively creating new practice, they are not professionals. Patrick Baccellieri models for us what true professionals do—they practice, above all; they work at the margins of established knowledge; they push that knowledge into practice; they work at solving the problems of social organization that connect knowledge to practice; they convert knowledge from an individual to a collective good; and they reflect on their work in ways that contribute to the knowledge of other practitioners. I, for one, hope that this book starts an avalanche of similarly detailed and disciplined analyses.

Richard F. Elmore, Ed.D.
Harvard University

Author of *School Reform from the Inside Out:
Policy, Practice, and Performance*

# Acknowledgements

I begin by thanking Ann Marie Ryan, my wife and fellow educator, for her interest in my work and support over the years while I served as a school principal, pursued my doctorate in urban educational leadership, and researched and wrote my thesis and this book. I also dedicate this book to my four children. A special thanks goes to my youngest, Julia, who was a toddler when I started this journey. She has expressed interest and curiosity while being patient with the reality that Daddy needed time to focus, work, and write.

I also thank my dissertation committee—Steve Tozer, Mark Smylie, Taffy Raphael, John Q. Easton, and Albert Bertani—for their support while I was a principal and during the experience of writing and defending my thesis. Especially, I thank my advisor and chair of my committee, Steve Tozer, for his guidance and mentorship during my doctoral studies. Thank you also to Joan Irwin, editor, for the thought and care that she brought to my book.

Finally, I thank the teachers, administrators, parents, students, community members, and external partners of South Loop Elementary School, many of whom worked tirelessly for a quality education. Without their persistence, hard work, and achievements, this book could not have been written.

*Professional Learning Communities: Using Data in Decision Making to Improve Student Learning* grew out of a case study I conducted of South Loop Elementary School in Chicago Public Schools. This study was informed by my work as the school's principal, my former experiences as an educator, and my current work as an administrator in the district office.

This story about South Loop begins with a description of the conditions at this once high-need urban elementary school, then discusses how the school's administration and teacher teams addressed these concerns, and concludes with descriptions of some of the accomplishments and lessons learned. Ultimately, this book is about how teachers learned to work with one another and engaged in common practices within and across grade-level teams. It is designed to show how the school leadership and teacher teams worked collaboratively to implement a great deal of reform over a relatively short period of time at a school that was historically resistant to change.

Plans were developed at South Loop to address issues and concerns about the school's culture, climate, teaching, and learning. The focus of this book is on the attention brought to teaching and learning, and specifically how South Loop used standardized and formative assessments to improve student learning in literacy. The systems and structures at the core of this work were new to most of the teachers at the school. Making change in practice is never easy. This book offers the opportunity to explore the school from the inside out and the outside in. You will read teachers' recollections about their experiences—some of which involved fear, resistance, courage, support, growth, learning, pride, and accomplishment.

This book demonstrates how South Loop's use of assessments and assessment data in assessment cycles contributed to school change. This work, grounded in the use of formative assessments, engaged teacher teams in the analysis of student assessment data, including student writing. On a regular basis, the school leadership team made time for the entire faculty and grade-level teams to analyze student work and discuss student reading, writing, and mathematics achievement data.

This cycle of assessment, data analysis, and data-driven curriculum planning and instruction influenced the quality and dynamic of the school's professional learning community, which developed strong teacher teams. This use of ongoing, schoolwide formative assessments provided a focus for the school community and became central to the work of teachers and students.

While the challenges at the school were significant, South Loop, a school that was once underperforming, made significant change. Not only did many of the students at the school improve in their ability to achieve as measured on standardized tests, but student behavior and the quality of student life at the school also improved.

Many teachers at the school experienced similar changes, resulting in improved collegiality and greater, deeper understanding about curriculum and instruction. Now, teachers at South Loop have supportive systems, structures, routines, and tools to overcome obstacles, and as a result, engage in high-quality teaching and learning.

These improvements attracted public attention, and the school has been featured a number of times in local news media as an example of school improvement. In fact, *The Chicago Tribune* referred to SLES as "the poster child" for school improvement in Chicago (Banchero November, 2005; *The Chicago Tribune* Editorial Board 2007). In October 2008, the Chicago Board of Education approved the opening of a new elementary school, South Shore Fine Arts Academy, based on the "South Loop Way." This new school will model its curriculum and administration on South Loop. To the principal at the new school, the "South Loop Way" means "collective responsibility" for student achievement (Maidenberg 2008).

After five years as the principal of South Loop, I made the decision to leave the school to work in the district's central office, where I have been working for two years. Initially I supported the work of the curriculum offices. Currently, I work as an administrator with the focus on improving the quality of teaching and learning in some of the district's most underperforming schools.

As a district administrator with Chicago Public Schools, I am very aware of our challenges. However, I know that when we work together, great things can happen. The case study of South Loop gave me the opportunity to reflect on some of the key work that took place in one school over five years and to understand the key factors that contributed to the school's success. Knowing that it takes a school community to develop a community school, I work with school principals, their schools, and neighborhood communities to dramatically improve the quality of the learning environment and teaching and learning at our schools. I know the challenges are significant and that, while it is important that there is a sense of coherence at the school, it is essential that multiple strategies be implemented in support of the desired change.

In August 2002, I remember walking into South Loop Elementary School for the first time, just two short weeks before the new school year was to begin. I had a sense of where things were and what needed to be accomplished; yet in the midst of it all, I saw the possibilities…a vibrant school community, teacher leadership, high degrees of collaboration, and most importantly, students with access and opportunities.

The story of South Loop illustrates that while the work at the school was built on a vision and mission, it took more than that to bring about changes at the school. At the core of this work was a focus on teachers—the continuous cycle of assessments, data analysis, and curriculum planning. Over time, teachers became accustomed to the structures, routines, expectations, and processes that facilitated collaboration. By themselves, these factors did not make a professional learning community. However, data shows that as these factors were implemented at South Loop, teacher use of assessments, data, and curriculum planning all increased and improved. These improvements brought about change and led to the development of a professional learning community.

# Chapter 1

# The Challenge of Change

The problem of student underachievement in reading continues to be a challenge for most urban school leaders and teachers. I became acutely aware of this challenge as principal of South Loop Elementary School in Chicago, Illinois. I was the principal there from August 2002 through June 2007. Throughout the school's history, and specifically during the six years preceding my arrival as principal, the school was a place of rapid and repeated administrative turnover and low student performance on standardized exams. Demographically, the school was composed of predominantly black students. The majority of the students qualified for Free and Reduced Lunch and were bussed to the school from nearby public housing.

My goal as principal was to work with the teachers to support them in strengthening instruction that would lead to improvements in student reading achievement. Because of the school's recent history, I was well aware of the obstacles the teachers faced, as well as those I had to confront in my attempts to build a professional learning community. Since I started as principal, the teachers and administration at South Loop have together brought about a great many changes.

These changes and how they were accomplished form the story that I tell in this book. Working together in a professional learning community, teachers and administrators became more observant about the meaning of assessment results and ways to improve student achievement. This story of South Loop provides a potential model that could be adapted to any school community and can help faculties become focused on improving student learning. Our experience demonstrates that teacher learning is the link between teacher conversation and student learning. In this model, teacher conversation is the domain for work-embedded professional development designed to bring focus to teaching and learning. Concentrating on what matters most results in the development of a *professional* learning community, not simply a learning community. Within this environment, South Loop teachers, literacy coaches, and administrators learned how to work with one another to improve the focus on teaching and learning by using common assessments and curriculum.

> "There is no such thing as an instant community, nor is there a single template for its form and content. It takes time for a community to take hold and for its members to develop effective ways to talk, think, and learn together."
>
> —Lieberman and Miller (2008, 12)

Through dialogue and collaboration, teachers learned to trust one another, their sense of self within the school changed, and their sense of collective responsibility increased. Teachers increased their expectations for themselves and one another, assumed added responsibility for improving the school, and felt responsible for helping each other to do their best so that all students would learn. Such achievements are not accomplished in the short term, nor can they be sustained without ongoing opportunities for teachers to collaborate and witness the beneficial results of their efforts. Over a period of five years, faculty at South Loop demonstrated that changing its culture and approach to curriculum and instruction produced significant improvements in student learning. These changes and their effects on student achievement continue at South Loop.

## History of South Loop Elementary School

South Loop Elementary School, a Chicago Public School located near the city's commercial center, was a place of controversy even prior to the opening of its doors in 1988 (Tanner 1988). Of 600 public elementary schools in Chicago, South Loop was one of the first to be built in an area of the city undergoing gentrification. Two years before the school opened, real estate developers promised middle class families moving into the school's attendance area that a new school would be part of the community. Low-income families in the Long Grove Homes, a subsidized apartment complex, and the Chicago Housing Authority's Hilliard Homes were also interested in enrolling their children in the school. While the desire for a quality education may have been the spark that moved families to lobby for access to the school, tensions around race and class emerged and the focus shifted away from education. These controversial matters dominated the school's agenda, preventing students from achieving academically. Decisions made by the Board of Education contributed to the problems because they did not please anyone. The Board intended for all interested families to come together and form one school community. The experiment was short-lived, and within three years, White, Asian, Hispanic, and Black middle class families either moved from the area or enrolled their children in other public or private schools.

Between 1990 and 1995, the school's demographics changed significantly. When the school opened, 25% of the 495 students were White and 70% of the students were Black. Within five years, 96% of the 546 students were Black. In 1990, 56% of the students were low-income students; by 1992, all the students were classified as low income. Academically, student reading achievement as reported on standardized tests paralleled the school's changing demographics. Schoolwide results were at their highest the first year that the school reported in 1990: 359 students were tested, and 26% demonstrated proficiency and were at or above national norms in reading achievement. In subsequent years, 22% to 16% of the students were at or above the national norms in reading comprehension. Students in third grade were consistently the lowest in student achievement out of the six grades tested each year. At least 85% of the students were not proficient in reading, as measured by the Iowa Tests of Basic Skills.

Low student achievement and demographic changes were not the only areas of concern for the neighborhood and the district. The school leadership was called into question. Between 1995 and 2002, South Loop experienced repeated turnover in administration, with six different principals serving over that period. The school's leadership was unable to resolve key issues within the school and in the community. As a result, most students in the neighborhood did not attend their neighborhood school.

The problems for South Loop continued and gained some media attention. In April 2002, a local paper characterized the school as a "sinking ship" and went on to report that "parents and neighbors worry about long-standing and still-unresolved problems at South Loop School" (Gibson 2002a, 1). The editor of the *Chicago Journal* claimed, "If the school is ever to become what it ought to be—an actual local school, drawing kids (and even well wishes) from the Dearborn Park area and beyond—the work… needs to be carried a step or two further. And the first and most important decision that the men and women of the next South Loop LSC [Local School Council]—elections are coming up in May—will face is who to hire as the school's next principal" (Gibson 2002b, 7).

> The perspective of a parent in a nearby neighborhood who chose to send his child to a private school highlighted a key challenge for the school: "The people in this neighborhood need to reclaim that school…but no one wants to fight that battle again, because of the firestorm. I understand the concerns of the parents from the Hilliard Homes, but they're not the ones paying for these property taxes."
> —Weissmann (1997, 2)

Local School Councils are one aspect of the decentralized system of the Chicago Public Schools (CPS). While it is not the role of the council to implement districtwide initiatives such as the Chicago Reading Initiative, LSCs are charged with hiring, evaluating, and retaining or firing a school principal. Under the 1988 Chicago School Reform Act, LSCs are authorized to hire principals and offer a four-year contract. If a principal leaves or is removed prior to the end of the contract, CPS central administration places an interim principal in the position. The principal works for both CPS and the LSC. Balancing local needs and district mandates can be complicated, but not impossible, in this decentralized configuration.

During the summer of 2002, CPS planned to place yet another interim principal at South Loop Elementary School. This decision could move the school forward or continue the patterns established in the school's culture. As the LSC geared up to hire a contract principal for November 2002, CPS was in the process of placing an interim principal to begin the 2002–2003 school year.

An article with the headline "Need for speed in principal search" reported on the status of the LSC's principal selection committee (Gibson 2002c, 1). The author reported that the committee had established a timeline and desired qualifications for their new principal. The article also described the progress on the selection of an interim principal to open the school year. It reported that CPS reviewed 66 of 100 applicants for the position and then narrowed the list to three. CPS requested the council's input on the placement of the interim principal. A subcommittee of the LSC interviewed the candidates and narrowed the list to two. With less than 30 days to the opening of the school, the committee planned to complete the process and "to get their recommendation to school officials posthaste" (Gibson 2002c, 3).

Collaboration around the hiring of the interim principal was an important step CPS took toward bridging the gap between the district and local management of the school. The district could have placed another interim principal in the school without input from the LSC. Often, interim principals are not accepted by the teachers, parents, or LSCs. An interim principal who is placed by CPS is usually labeled the "Board's pick"—someone to push an agenda. As a result, one big hurdle for an interim principal is the issue of trust. With the interview process for a contract principal in the planning stages for this school, building trust at an early stage of involvement was critical to bringing continuity to the school.

I was selected as the school's interim principal in August 2002. Subsequently, in November 2002, I was selected to lead the school as the contract principal. In the spring of 2002, the Board of Education passed policies to start two new instructional programs at the school for 2003: an Early Childhood Center and Regional Gifted Center. Both of these programs had the potential to attract new families to the school, ideally families from within the school's attendance area. Yet, as the school's history had shown, introducing new programs prior to any noticeable changes at the school might result in little improvement.

Even before accepting the interim appointment, I was well aware of the magnitude of the task facing me. I knew that the majority of third- through eighth-grade students demonstrated below-proficiency performance on reading assessments, as well as on the State Board of Education's Illinois Standardized Achievement Test. Declining enrollment and school segregation were other significant challenges. The recent instability of the school's administration and staff presented additional challenges. Some of the persistent conditions of the school included high teacher autonomy, serious student behavior problems, and controversies within the community. At the outset, I knew that I had to demonstrate my resolve and commitment to improve the conditions in the school so that teachers and students could all achieve success, and that members of the community would see these positive results and would want to have their children attend South Loop.

## Factors Related to Change in Schools

The circumstances at South Loop are likely similar to those that other educators have experienced in urban schools. Student underachievement and mobility, declining enrollments, and changing demographics combined with administrative instability and teacher burnout and turnover create situations that are ripe for change. School reform literature and policies provide approaches and solutions for addressing problems related to student underachievement. Three areas of school reform in large urban districts have particular application for the developments that occurred at South Loop: school-level change, standards-based curriculum and instruction, and development of a professional learning community. This literature helps us to understand how districts or schools with cultures entrenched in mistrust, fear, and underachievement have successfully engaged in reform efforts, developed collaborative school learning communities, and made positive gains in student achievement.

> Changing teaching practices "...is a problem of enhancing individual knowledge and skill, not a problem of organizational structure; getting the structures right depends on first understanding that problem of knowledge and skill."
>
> —Elmore et al. (1996, 240)

The literature on school-level reform presents multiple studies on the complexities of school-level change, specifically school infrastructure arguments. Changes in school leadership can potentially resolve tensions between keeping things intact and pushing for change. As the incoming principal at South Loop, I realized that I would likely face such tensions and would have to develop ways to affect change that would foster the support of the teachers and the community. Shared leadership is an important factor in accomplishing change—the school is strengthened when there is control at the school level and, by implication, among school leaders and teachers. To overcome challenges when new policies are enacted, schools and teachers must have the resources and knowledge base to respond effectively. This situation requires restructuring schools so that teachers have time to meet and that the students have opportunities to learn. However, the research also reveals that such restructuring alone will not help.

Standards-based curriculum provides the framework within which school leaders and teachers can address problems in student achievement. For my part, I had to find out how teachers at South Loop thought about curriculum, how they focused on state standards, and how they used information about student performance to shape instruction. Some questions that captured my immediate attention included: Did the school follow a standards-based curriculum? Did teachers use research-based instructional strategies? Was there continuity in the curriculum across the grades? Did teachers share mutual expectations for student achievement? To what extent was the community aware of the curriculum and the expectations the curriculum set for students? I recognized that none of these learning expectations could be addressed or realized without the full participation of the teachers.

"I believe collaboration is the only way you're ever going to have the fundamental change you need for teachers to really talk about how they're going to help students become more successful. You've got to give teachers the time to work together, to work on things like common assessments and teaching strategies, and to talk about results."

—Jeffers cited in Von Frank (2008, 6)

The nature of relationships among the adults within a school is another critical factor related to the success of reform efforts. Schools must have a safe environment in which teachers can share strategies, beliefs, and practices. Such schools are understood as democratic organizations guided by ethics and positive values. They are also grounded in collaborative or transformational leadership practices. These attributes of professional learning communities are laudable and likely to have most teachers and school leaders readily subscribe to them. However, the circumstances at South Loop, with its recent history of rapid and repeated administrative turnover, indicated to me that the foundations for a professional learning community most likely were not in place. This observation reminded me of the argument that underperforming urban schools possess entrenched cultures that have significant barriers to change. Such schools face a complicated dilemma. Schools need to be safe and collaborative in order for student achievement to thrive, yet underperforming schools significantly lack these characteristics and qualities.

Numerous reforms and approaches mentioned in the literature illustrate key concerns about inequitable practices leading to student underachievement and a real desire to address this problem. However, some of the literature argues that in order to make significant change in the culture of a school, more than one reform strategy must be implemented in order for reform to take hold. To address the significant student learning and achievement needs, reform ought to not only address the structural and organizational aspects of reform, but address also levers for change in the curriculum, instruction, and culture of the school. The task may seem overwhelming for some districts and schools, but it is important to note that an all-encompassing reform framework is critical in order to address the complexities in the school. There are successful initiatives that point to such comprehensive approaches; yet the literature identifies problems, and what should happen in schools is not clear. The technical aspects of change and improvement are missing. In writing about my experience at South Loop, I hope to offer this procedural knowledge by providing descriptions of key forces of the reform and how a school moved from its low-performing status within a complicated policy environment.

## Overview of Student Reading Achievement at South Loop

South Loop reported significant gains in student achievement over a relatively short period of time. Figure 1.1 shows the school's demographics and results in reading (percentage of students meeting or exceeding the standards) on the Illinois Standards Achievement Test (ISAT), 2001–2007.

**Figure 1.1. South Loop School Demographics and ISAT Reading Proficiency Results, Grades 3–8**

| Year | 2001 | 2002 | 2003 | 2004 | 2005 | 2006 | 2007 |
|---|---|---|---|---|---|---|---|
| Students not qualifying for F&RL | 21 | 9 | 19 | 10 | 27 | 79 | 138 |
| Students qualifying for F&RL | 141 | 119 | 88 | 90 | 71 | 111 | 81 |
| ISAT for students not qualifying for F&RL | 47.6% | n/a^ | 47.4% | 40.0% | 77.8% | 83.5% | 85.5% |
| ISAT for students qualifying for F&RL | 29.1% | 30.3% | 28.4% | 50.0% | 45.1% | 74.8% | 75.3% |

Source: ISAT Overtime, 2007

F&RL = Free and Reduced Lunch

^Achievement data is not released by the district if there are fewer than 10 students.

While there is no question that student performance on standardized tests sharply improved at South Loop during this period, a number of questions remain about the exact contributors to that change. As one University of Illinois at Chicago faculty observer commented, "If you could bottle it, you could sell it," which is a shorthand way of saying that we don't completely understand the complexities of what went on at South Loop to bring about the improvements that have attracted attention. For example, it is widely believed that adjustments in the format and administration of the ISAT in 2006 may have contributed to increased student scores throughout Chicago and among lower-performing schools throughout Illinois. But South Loop scores improved well beyond the scores of other schools in Chicago and well beyond the likely test effects of the new ISAT.

Moreover, as illustrated in Figure 1.1, South Loop scores on ISAT had been notable for their improvement in the three years prior to 2006.

The change in demographics between 2003 and 2007 is another factor complicating explanations for the improvement in student achievement. Because family income is such a strong predictor of standardized test results, some observers attributed achievement improvements to the changing demographics. Free and Reduced Lunch (F&RL) is the primary indicator of socioeconomic status. However, inspection of Figure 1.1 reveals that students at South Loop qualifying for F&RL in 2003 and 2004 demonstrated stronger test gains than students not qualifying for F&RL who attended the school during this time. Students qualifying for F&RL scored 28.4% on ISAT during 2003 and 50% in 2004. Students not qualifying for F&RL scored 47.4 % on ISAT in 2003 and 40% in 2004.

Other data also show that there was not a significant increase of students tested who did not qualify for F&RL during 2002 through 2005, when the school made a considerable increase in student achievement. These student numbers fluctuate: 19 students during 2003, 10 students during 2004, and 27 students during 2005. Prior to the reform (2001), 21 students were tested who did not qualify for F&RL, showing that there were more nonqualifying SES students tested during that year than during 2004 when the school made its increase in achievement. Setting the numbers of students tested aside, there are almost parallel gains for students in both economic categories over a five-year period, 2003 through 2007. Students qualifying for F&RL moved from 28.4% meeting or exceeding reading standards during 2003 to 75.3% meeting or exceeding the standards in 2007—an increase of 46.9 percentage points. Students not qualifying for F&RL moved from 47.4% meeting or exceeding the reading standards during 2003 to 85.5% meeting or exceeding the standards during 2007, increasing 38.1 percentage points.

While some observers perceived that demographic shifts may have affected overall student performance during the period from 2003 through 2007, and that test changes are likely to have affected increased school performance in 2006, there is sufficient evidence that other factors influenced student performance during this time. But what were those influences? The changes in student performance at this time were accompanied by changes for the teachers in the use of assessment tools and curriculum resources, as well as participation in a professional learning community. Research about the centrality of classroom instruction in improving learning is convincing (DuFour and Eaker 1998; Hopkins and Reynolds 2001; Elmore 2002). Consequently, my belief is that one important factor influencing student performance was the quality of curriculum and instruction at South Loop. Accordingly, I also believe that this factor influenced the decision of the neighborhood's middle-income parents to enroll their children in increasing numbers at the school. While the faculty was forming a professional learning community with the goal of improving student achievement, the community began to recognize and appreciate the changes occurring at South Loop.

## Meeting Challenges Through Collaboration

The experiences at South Loop provide insights into the change process that led from a comparatively nonsystematic and incoherent approach to curriculum and instruction to an intentional, systematic, and coherent approach. The remaining chapters reveal what South Loop administrators, teachers, and literacy coaches learned as they collaborated in examining student work, sharing information about instructional practices, and reflecting on their professional knowledge and growth. I hope this story of one school's transformation sheds light on what is critical for school leaders, teachers, researchers, and policymakers to know and do as we focus on changing the trends in urban school reform.

## Reflection: Thinking About Teaching and Learning

1. From the chapter, select one quotation that best represents your perspective about the challenge of change. Share your observations about the quotation with colleagues, or jot down some thoughts in your professional learning journal.

2. Think about efforts at change that you have experienced throughout your career. What factors or situations prompted these efforts at change? How do these factors compare to those described for South Loop Elementary School?

3. How would you describe your experiences with change efforts? What impact did these experiences have (or continue to have) on your views of teaching, student learning, and professional development?

# Chapter 2

# Complexities of School-Level Change

My case study of how South Loop Elementary School changed its culture and its approach to curriculum and instruction reveals the range of demands that educators face as they strive to improve teaching and learning. As the principal involved in the reform at this particular school, the study was a way for me to examine and describe what occurred and why. The study centers on how South Loop's use of standardized and formative assessments improved student learning in literacy. The school, easily identified by many in Chicago, is known as a place where a great deal of change took place and where reform was effective. From a distance, some give credit for the school's reform to a changing neighborhood and new families at the school, believing that newly enrolled students from middle- and upper-socioeconomic backgrounds brought improvements in student achievement. However, as the school's history illustrates, middle- and upper-income racially diverse families did not enroll their children in this urban school when it was segregated, labeled as troubled, and underperforming. In short, the school's change and significant increase in student achievement raised questions and also demonstrated what may be possible across the city as well as in other schools and districts.

## Developing a Case Study of School-Level Change

Case study research provides an opportunity for the researcher to examine closely, even become immersed in, a particular situation or culture in order to better understand a particular issue or problem. As South Loop's principal for five years, I was in a position to preserve records of real-life events—a condition of effective case study research that Yin (2003) describes as value-added. Furthermore, it is the legal responsibility of the school principal to retain records and to submit reports in order to document the school's history and provide the statements or records that may be used in a court of law.

While this access to data could strengthen a school's case study conducted by its former principal, there are also weaknesses to it. However, this is true for any researcher in that records could be altered or reinterpreted to shape the desired results of a study, or that former employees and others who are interviewed could be swayed to recite specific events of stories just to appease their former employer. A researcher who was also the school's principal could be *capable* of case study research in the same school, but it was critical that the research methodology be sound and the researcher ethical. Safeguards needed to be put in place.

With this in mind, it is important for me to clarify a few important points. While I served as the school's principal for five years, in June 2007, I accepted a district-level position with Chicago Public Schools. Therefore, though I exercised a great deal of influence over most aspects of the school while I was the principal, this was not the case during the time that I conducted the study. In addition, I decided that the best way to proceed for the majority of the data collection was to follow practices similar to conducting a study at one's place of work. Therefore, documents generated from regular practices in the workplace constitute the source for the majority of data for this case study. I used independent focus groups to obtain comments from teachers and coaches who participated in the events described in this study. As a result, I conducted this study in a way that was authentic to case study research. I am committed to and concerned about urban education and have sought to develop a clear picture of what occurred as we worked to increase teaching and learning.

Based on my experience at South Loop, I argue that the nation's children and families do not need to wait another generation for school change to take place. My research provides evidence to support the claim that it is critical that school leaders focus on developing a comprehensive framework for reform aimed at improving teaching and learning, which in turn leads to improved student achievement.

While this framework must embrace increasing academic and behavioral expectations that are at least equal to the life and academic challenges that students face, it must also include a focus on changing the school's culture. In so doing, the youth of today could have greater opportunities for developing foundations for success in the day-to-day realities of schools, and in turn, opening doors to future options and choices.

This framework is defined by five core principles, each of which is supported in the literature on curricular reform:

1. **Improve student learning by improving classroom instruction.** Focusing on and investing in developing teachers' skill and knowledge strengthens their practice which, in turn, produces improvements in student learning (DuFour and Eaker 1998; Elmore 2002; Hopkins and Reynolds 2001).

2. **Improve classroom instruction through teacher learning of new knowledge, skills, and dispositions (attitudes, habits of thought, etc.).** Long-term staff development is essential for change to take place in teaching and learning (Au and Hirata 2005; Dutro et al. 2002; Joyce and Showers 2002; Taylor et al. 2005).

3. **Support teacher learning through professional learning communities.** School-based teacher learning communities are critical for continuous and improved student achievement (DuFour and Eakers 1998; Hubbard, Mehan, and Stein 2006; McLaughlin and Talbert 2003). Similarly, Sebring et al. (2006) and Wagner et al. (2006) argue that schools grounded in concepts of professional learning communities are more likely to show substantial improvements.

4. **Structure professional learning communities by providing teachers with the time and resources to discuss student learning outcomes and how to improve those outcomes.** The resultant teacher learning is likely to benefit student learning if teachers are encouraged and supported in their efforts to change classroom practices (DuFour and Eakers 1998; Elmore 2002; Grossman and Wineberg 2000; Hopkins and Reynolds 2001).

5. **Encourage shared discussion of standards-based formative assessments, including student writing, conducted in a professional learning community supported by multiple systems and structures, which can lead to changes in classroom practice.** Instruction is designed to implement effective practices that are in turn designed to meet individual student learning. Reform ought to promote smart, short-term cycles of action, assessment, and adjustment—activities at the core of a professional learning community (Schmoker 2004). Improving formative assessment practices can raise teaching expectations and standards, leading to increased student achievement (Black et al. 2004; Boudett et al. 2005). Effective use of student assessment data can lead to change in teaching practices (Sharkey and Murnane 2006; Wayman and Stringfield 2006; Young 2006). Taylor et al. (in press) maintain that literacy achievement can improve through teacher ownership in the implementation of schoolwide reform in response to increased or higher standards.

Taken together, these principles describe conditions necessary for responsible Standards-Based Change (sometimes referred to as SBC), a process which, at the school level, is a time-consuming, meticulous process of reflection and action (Raphael et al. in press). The story about the change that took place at South Loop illustrates the point made about the conditions for responsible standards-based change. While many in the field of education affirm that the key principles stated above are important, it is *how* they are implemented that will make all the difference when it comes to school change. At South Loop, teachers worked together to learn how to discuss formative assessment data with their grade-level teams, as well as in schoolwide forums. School change began to take place when teams of teachers worked together to navigate this work.

## Standards-Based Curriculum and Instruction

Standards can provide coherence to instruction across grade levels in a school; however, the degree to which coherence is achieved depends on the extent to which teachers are aware of and attentive to the standards. Early on in working with the teachers at South Loop, I set out to discover to what extent standards were featured in their planning and instruction. One teacher recalls these initial discussions:

> **Teacher:** *The principal talked to us in a meeting about [standards-based] change and nobody knew what it was about. None of us were recent college graduates. At the time, the faculty was kind of an older faculty and so the people weren't familiar with this at all. We...never had a student teacher, and we weren't really having a lot of young teachers at the time.*
>
> *And we just had all these different programs that were never followed through on anything and we just thought: 'Oh, what's this?' And [the administration] had just talked to us about it in a meeting and we just sat, slightly listening, thinking that nothing would ever come of it—we didn't know that he was really...committed to it. ...we didn't know.*

"Engaging teachers in shared examination of multiple sources of data on their students' achievement provides an environment for teachers to learn about the learning needs of students, thus making collaborative planning about improved curriculum, instruction, and assessment more likely."
—Baccellieri (2009, 59)

The field of curriculum and instruction is filled with differing opinions, practices, studies, and theories, some of which can attest to improvements in student learning and achievement. Although the literature reports that learning standards and outcomes are somewhat controversial, I maintain that examination of this literature helps build understanding of how schools and districts use standards to engage teachers and students in curriculum and instruction. Many of the themes I discovered in the literature resonated with my experiences at South Loop. Examples that are particularly pertinent to my case study are discussed in the next sections of this chapter.

## Processes for Standards-Based Change

Elmore (2002) argues that standards-based school reform is critical to the types of change that are needed in urban schools. In a paper discussing the importance of professional development in school reform, he claims that continuous improvement is the course that will shift schools from how they have been traditionally perceived. "The question is whether other school systems, operating in an environment of increased attention to student performance and quality of instruction, will discover that they need to learn not just different ways of doing things, but very different ways of thinking about the purposes of their work, and the skills and knowledge that go with those purposes" (Elmore 2002, 35). The core of school change and reform centers on a critical problem: "how to construct relatively orderly ways for people to engage in activities that have as their consequence the learning of new ways to think about and do their jobs, and how to put these activities in the context of reward structures that stimulate them to do more of what leads to large scale improvement and less of what reinforces the pathologies of the existing structure" (Elmore 2002, 36).

Similarly, Falk (2000) saw the need to develop a structure and system grounded in standards. Based on years of experience as a school-based educator and researcher, Falk's work is designed to make sense of the complex issues that are involved in standards-based education, to explain concerns of the various perspectives, and to offer a pathway for how to proceed. By using standards and assessments, teachers can keep learning at the center of curriculum: "keeping the image of learning in mind as we work with standards to develop curriculum is a potent reminder that our teaching task is not merely about covering standards" (Falk 2000, 104). Falk further notes that "curriculum is often constructed under the assumption that learners have no impact on plans" (Falk 2000, 104). On the contrary, it is essential for teachers to use evidence to guide teaching, as the data provide necessary details about what is critical to ensure that students learn key concepts.

Falk's study provides a compelling argument for establishing a schoolwide process for using standards and assessments to build coherence in a school. This process could include such activities as developing rubrics for standards-based assessment, reviewing student work samples in teams, and also working to collaboratively score student work (Falk 2000, 108). Falk observes that "working with performance assessments offers teachers exactly these kinds of opportunities for professional learning" (2000, 131).

Improving reading achievement was a primary focus for reform at South Loop. Consequently, I looked to resources that examined how teacher instruction and school organizational factors affect the reading achievement of urban primary students. In this context, I examined case studies of 14 high-poverty urban schools across the United States (Taylor et al. 2000). The schools involved in the study either adopted an external school reform program to improve reading achievement or developed programs from within the school. As a result of the findings from these case studies, the researchers recommended that schools consider reform efforts that supported both instructional practices and school organization. A particular feature of this research is the contribution it makes to effective practices for teaching reading in high-poverty urban schools. These practices include active responding, small-group instruction, and higher-level questions (Taylor et al. 2002).

The CIERA (Center for the Improvement of Early Reading Achievement) School Change Framework provided structure to and support for school improvement in reading (Taylor et al. 2005). This approach to school improvement centered on a framework for change that was described as "homegrown"—a situation in which it was observed that "teachers' collaboration, teachers' decisions about what to study, and teachers' perseverance made the difference in the more successful schools" (Taylor et al. 2005, 66). In my study, I examined changes among South Loop teachers and literacy coaches as they participated in various activities where they worked together to make data-based decisions about instruction. The results at South Loop were consistent with those described in the CIERA school change research.

Au and Hirata (2005) also addressed improved teaching and learning through teacher leadership and professional development while reflecting on their involvement with school change in response to higher standards. The Standards-Based Change Process provides a roadmap that districts and schools can use to initiate and sustain efforts to improve student achievement in literacy. This process, shown in Figure 2.1, includes a "To Do List" that encompasses nine interrelated features: philosophy, vision of an excellent reader, grade-level or department benchmarks, "I can" statements, evidence, procedures for collecting evidence, rubrics, bar graphs (to display evidence), and instructional improvements.

**Figure 2.1. The Standards-Based Change Process To Do List**

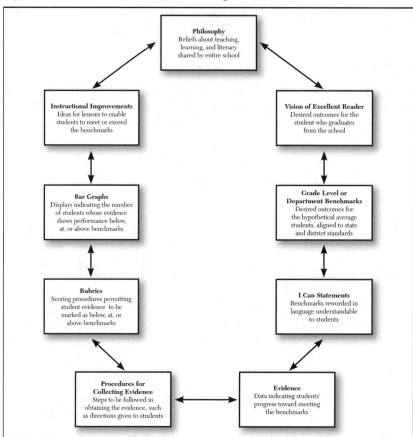

Source: From Au, K. A. and S. Y. Hirata. (2005). Negotiating the Slippery Slope: School Change and Literacy Achievement. *Journal of Literacy Research*, 37(3).

The Standards-Based Change Process provides a comprehensive approach to school reform. The results must not only involve teachers in a process but also lead them to a product—improved student achievement (Au and Hirata 2005, 281). Furthermore, Au and Hirata maintain that higher test scores equal the degree to which schools effectively implement the steps or stages of the Standards-Based Change Process. Seven developmental levels constitute this process (Taylor, Raphael, and Au in press). These levels advance from individual or small-group awareness of a need through full engagement of all stakeholders in the school community. Throughout the process, members of the school faculty become more involved in constructing the building blocks for change, taking into account assessment data, instructional benchmarks, and instructional decisions.

I have indicated that improving students' reading achievement was a primary objective for school change efforts at South Loop. According to Au, Hirata, and Raphael (2005), literacy achievement can improve through schoolwide reform work in the standards. The authors identify problems faced by schools as they attempt to improve teaching and learning—pressures for quick improvement in student achievement, external accountability, incoherent curriculum, and lack of focused curriculum. Citing significant improvements in student achievement on state assessments at Kipapa Elementary School in Mililani, Hawaii and at South Loop, Au and her colleagues build a strong case for the benefits of following the Standards-Based Change Process. This process can foster change and development in a school's curriculum and instruction, as well as in a school's professional learning community. These changes lead to improved student achievement. Acknowledging that not all schools involved in the process produced significant test results, Au et al. observe that impressive results can be seen in schools committed in a disciplined way to improving student learning in literacy. Having a well-defined process for change was clearly helpful to South Loop leadership and teachers. We not only knew what we wanted to accomplish, but we also had the means available to reach that goal.

Working with standards enables teachers to become more focused on the how, what, and why of instruction that fosters students' learning as well as motivation. School-based initiatives that involve teachers collaboratively examining standards, curriculum, and student performance can strengthen professionalism. Standards-based curriculum and instruction was central to the experiences of teachers and administration at South Loop as we endeavored to create a learning environment in which all students could achieve success.

## Assessment Practices

Student achievement at South Loop was a major concern. As previously mentioned, historically over 65% of students in grades three through eight demonstrated below-proficiency performance on the Illinois Standardized Achievement Test. Reading achievement, one of the main areas of focus for the school, was in particular need of improvement. Determining the factors affecting student performance led to exploration of assessment practices in the school. Two questions about assessment are central to the case study of change at South Loop:

1. What systems and structures were established to support the use of assessments and assessment data?
2. What role did assessments and assessment data play in teacher meetings and professional development sessions?

An examination of the professional literature on assessment practices provided insights that enabled me to better understand and appreciate how South Loop teachers dealt with assessment challenges.

> "Standards-based reforms can help support a new vision of teaching, one that weaves teaching, learning, and assessment into a seamless web. This linkage of standards, assessments, and teaching practices can provide a guide for teachers and students to use in monitoring and taking responsibility for their own learning."
>
> —Falk (2002, 619)

## High-Stakes Assessment

Assessment, particularly high-stakes assessment, has been a dominant issue in educational policy and practice most notably since passage of the No Child Left Behind Act in 2000. The Act resulted in districts and schools paying more attention to accountability for improving student achievement and how they assess progress. Such attention also raised questions about the effect of high-stakes tests on teaching and learning. Stiggins identified the limitations of standardized tests and advised that "for assessment to become truly useful, politicians, school leaders, and society in general must come to understand the gross *insufficiency* of these tests as a basis for assessment for school improvement" (2004, 23). Although standardized tests do provide some evidence of student achievement, the data are not sufficient to guide changes in teaching practice. Furthermore, as Amrein and Berliner (2002; 2003) reported, such tests are often accompanied by such negative outcomes as reduced achievement, increased dropout rates, and reduced graduation rates—especially for minority students. Their research supports the notion that high-stakes testing programs do not necessarily improve the quality of teaching and learning. Teachers are well aware that the results of annual state tests provide too little information and arrive too late for planning instruction.

## Formative Assessment

Recognizing the limitations of standardized tests, other researchers have explored formative assessment with a view to demonstrating ways in which assessment, teaching, and learning are reciprocal activities. These efforts provide additional insights into factors that may contribute to school-level change. Heritage defines formative assessment as "a systematic process to continuously gather evidence about learning" (2007, 141). A wide range of strategies apply to formative assessment, any of which allow teachers and students to become more aware of what constitutes effective learning.

Formative assessment practices provide additional insights into factors that may bring about school-level change. Citing a 1998 review of over 250 internationally published articles, Black, Harrison, Lee, Marshall, and Wiliam claim that "improving formative assessments raises standards" and increases student achievement. However, this initial study provided little evidence about effective practices for teacher implementation (2004, 9). Subsequently, Black et al. (2004) developed several projects in which they worked with teachers to develop innovative classroom practices that focused on the concept of assessment for learning. The authors note, "Assessment for learning is any assessment for which the first priority in its design and practice is to serve the purpose of promoting students' learning" (2004, 10). The formative nature of assessment comes into play when "the evidence is actually used to adapt the teaching work to meet learning needs" (2004, 10). Specifically, the researchers examined four aspects of classroom work: questioning, feedback through grading, peer- and self-assessment, and the formative use of summative tests. Based on the results from these studies, Black et al. assert that collaboration with others who are trying out similar innovations will provide support as teachers using formative assessments work to increase expectations and change classroom cultures. Notably, through participation in the studies, both researchers and teachers acknowledged that the changes stemming from improved assessment practices enabled them to reflect on deeper issues about teaching and learning.

Formative assessment is particularly valuable to teachers because it is allied with instruction that facilitates immediate and ongoing observation of learning. Seeking lessons learned from one large urban school district's implementation of a formative assessment system, Sharkey and Murnane maintained that teachers and administrators need access to formative assessment data that can be used without delay. They concluded that ease and timeliness for use of data in schools is essential in order to create a "culture of learning from student assessment results" (2006, 586).

The development and use of formative assessments and assessment data was at the core of our work at South Loop. Standards and formative assessment go hand in hand; consequently, it was necessary for the teachers to learn about standards-based learning outcomes and assessment routines that reflected the level of rigor expected to meet the demands of the outcomes. Additionally, the teachers learned to develop a way to score student performance on that assessment. Since the school was focused on a standards-based approach to teaching and learning, the formative assessments were narrowly focused on key tasks and proficiencies for writing and for reading comprehension. Descriptions of how we used standards-based formative assessments are provided in Chapter 4.

### Processes for Examining Assessment Data

Cognizant of the demands for high-stakes accountability in the context of standards and No Child Left Behind requirements, a team consisting of school leaders from three Boston public schools, doctoral students, and faculty from the Harvard Graduate School of Education met to determine effective practices. Boudett, City, and Murnane argue that "analyzing a variety of student assessment results can contribute to fulfilling their goals, if careful attention is paid to the limitations of tests and the technical challenges to interpreting student responses" (2005, 3). Using this approach, this reform chose to utilize student data from mandated external or state tests or assessments. Additional data was sought from internal sources at the classroom and school level from writing prompts, unit tests, and science fairs to name a few.

As a result of working together for over a two-year period, Boudett et al. (2005) developed the Data Wise Improvement Process, designed to provide a guide or road map for organizing and utilizing assessment results. The improvement cycle consists of eight steps: organize for collaborative work, build assessment literacy, create data overview, dig into student data, examine instruction, develop an action plan, plan to assess progress, and act and assess (Boudett et al. 2006, 1). Prepare, inquire, and act are the sequence of activities that teachers engage in as they work through the Data Wise Improvement Process. This improvement cycle ends where it began, with the initial criteria or expectations for what was to be achieved. Now, at the end of the cycle, or the beginning of a new cycle, these expectations are reviewed. Incremental increases are made where necessary, creating a cycle of continuous improvement. See Figure 2.2 below.

**Figure 2.2. Data Wise Improvement Process**

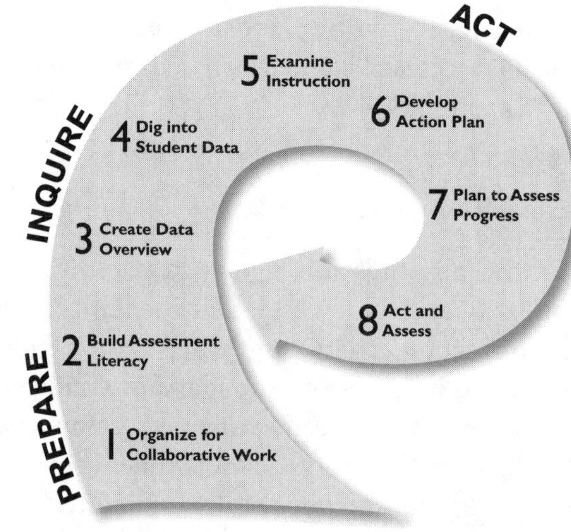

Source: Reprinted with permission from *Data Wise: A Step-by-Step Guide to Using Assessment Results to Improve Teaching and Learning*, edited by Katheyn Parker Boudett, Elizabeth A. City, and Richard J. Murname, (Cambridge, MA: Harvard Education Press, 2005), p. 5. For more information, please visit www.harvardeducationpress.org, or call 1-888-437-1437.

The work of Boudett and her colleagues represents a coherent approach to effective use of assessment for school improvement. The Data Wise approach addresses process aspects of implementation, as well as the specifics of data analysis. By drawing on high-stakes tests and internal assessments as primary data sources, this process provides continuity between external and internal assessments. This integrated use of the state standards, high-stakes external tests, and internal assessments serves to organize a coherent curriculum (Boudett et al. 2005, 131). Successful implementation of the Data Wise process centers on the effectiveness of teacher discussions on student data. For school leaders working in situations where there is a low relational trust among colleagues, inability to move through such obstacles would significantly impair the process. Nonetheless,

Boudett et al. argue that an effective school has "a community of adults committed to working together to develop the skills and knowledge of all children" (2005, 3).

## Use of Assessment Data

Teachers' understanding of what constitutes data and the impact of the organizational setting on their use of data is another area of research into assessment practices. Using case study research, Young (2006) determined that the norms and values that are imbedded in a particular school, department, and/or grade-level team will play a significant role in how teachers understand and utilize data as an improvement strategy. Other factors that affect the progress in a school's ability to use data adequately include district and school agenda setting, teacher leadership, and cohesiveness across departments or grade levels. Young maintains that recognition of these factors is not sufficient to accomplish needed change in the use of assessment data. Implementing such change requires leaders to provide data-management systems, provide training to help teachers become fluent in their use of data, and also facilitate processes to shift norms and values so that the use of data will be a meaningful exercise for teachers, leading to improvement in teaching and learning.

While not making claims of causal relationships among teachers' use of student data, teaching practice, and student achievement, Wayman and Stringfield argue that teachers "...felt the improvement in their practice benefited students and led to improved student learning, and administrators cited increased test scores" (2006, 554). In a study of the use of student data systems at three experienced schools, Wayman and Stringfield sought to advance facultywide involvement in the use of student data systems as an avenue to improved teaching practices. One question explored in this study was "What changes in faculty practice and attitudes have resulted from the use of these software tools to examine and learn from student data?" (2006, 554).

While this study is not intended to illustrate how schools and teachers who are unfamiliar with data have changed and adopted data-driven practices or improved their professional learning community, Wayman and Stringfield (2006) claim that as a result of using current and historical student assessment data, teachers saw their own practice as improved. In addition, Wayman and Stringfield argue that it is critical that data is used for school improvement and that a school's nonthreatening use of data is essential. These approaches or attitudes will better lead to teachers' trust that data will not be used against them. As a result of how the three schools used data, Wayman and Stringfield claim that teachers reported improved "conversations among educators, administrators, and parents" and they believed that they were better able to use differentiated and collaborative teaching methods (2006, 568). Understanding change in teachers' conversations was an important feature of my case study. As you will see in Chapter 5, teachers' conversations were central to the change efforts at South Loop.

The struggles teachers encounter with adopting new forms of assessment have attracted researchers' attention. In this context, Earl and Katz claim that teachers are likely to hold intuitive beliefs about how students learn, which guide how they teach, and that these beliefs are critical to their relationship to the curriculum and the learner. The researchers claimed that how teachers teach and how they assess were inevitably based on their visions of competence and beliefs about how to help students learn. They observed that "most teachers vacillated back and forth from the familiar to the new, reverting to the traditional 'when it really counted'" (2000, 110). This study illustrates the challenges for school leaders and policy makers in making effective changes in teacher practices that will make a difference for student learning and achievement.

Changes in assessment practices at South Loop involved the teachers in new ways of thinking about what they taught, how they taught, and how they determined what their students were learning. Our accomplishments in using formative assessments to support standards-based change were consistent with several themes in the literature on assessment. Specifically, it is useful to note the following:

- Improving formative assessment practices can raise teaching expectations and standards, leading to increased student achievement.

- Integrated use of standards, high-stakes external tests, and internal formative assessments serve to organize a coherent curriculum, the foundation for increasing student achievement.

- Commitment to sustained school improvement and long-term reform efforts must engage teachers in developing meaningful products that are at the core of teaching and learning.

- Change in teaching and learning occur when teachers see their own practice as improved through their use of student assessment data.

- Teachers' direct and ongoing involvement in assessment processes fosters ownership in the implementation of schoolwide reform.

This case study exemplifies application of strong theoretical concepts that are critical for schools to improve. Many teachers who hear about school change want to know how the effort affected the teachers who were involved. What did it feel like for teachers at these schools to "raise teaching experiences" or to engage in "formative assessment practices"? These concerns are very real. When teachers change assessment practices and when they focus on standards to define learning outcomes, they change the way they teach. However, such change cannot occur without institutional supports that enable teachers to get together for the expressed purposes of building their knowledge and skills about teaching and learning. Grade-level team meetings, scheduled during the school day, were one form of support for South Loop teachers. It would have been next to impossible for South Loop to make the type of school change that was made without the time and structure for teachers to work together.

> "Data-driven decision making does not simply require good data; it also requires good decisions."
> —Hess (2009, 17)

## Professional Learning Communities

Teacher engagement is a concept embedded in research and programs related to school-level change. This concept is evident throughout the previous descriptions of standards-based curriculum and assessment practices—the extent to which teachers embrace the content and processes of change has a significant impact on the success of reforms. The critical role of teachers in contributing to decisions about using standards, creating a coherent curriculum, and drawing on data to shape instruction has gained momentum in recent years. Professional learning communities have become central to initiating and sustaining effective school reform. When I became principal at South Loop, I was well aware that it would not be possible to create needed changes in the school without the willing support of the teachers. I also understood that individuals might hold conflicting views about change within the school and its role within the community. Given the history of the school, I recognized that building an environment that fostered collegial trust and respect was essential if other achievements were to be realized. The recollections of two literacy coaches about how they collaborated when they were teachers prior to 2003 offer a picture of the situation:

> **Literacy Coach 2:** *Both [of us] were here like seven years before [the new administration] came. We did not have any regularly scheduled grade-level meetings. That was a new concept to like meet with our peers. So we definitely said yes, we'd like to meet at this time, and this time it did not happen.*
>
> *[The idea of grade-level meetings] was overwhelming…because [prior to the new administration] we would like meet in the hallways…and [ask] what do you want to do.*
>
> **Literacy Coach 1:** *Yeah, right. Right. Just general discussions about what are you going to do about this or how do you do this?*
>
> **Literacy Coach 2:** *But for the most part, I mean, it was very much, you come in. You go into your classroom. You shut your door. You teach what you want to teach, and you teach what's in the book, and then you dismiss your kids and then you do the same thing again.*

These individuals had experienced working in isolation, an ingrained and accepted practice in many schools. Such a condition can be a formidable foe to overcome in efforts to accomplish school-level change. However, agents of change cannot let themselves be intimidated by such situations; through their actions they must demonstrate personal and professional commitment to supporting and encouraging teachers as they embark on collaborative activities. As Elmore observes, "schools and school systems that are improving directly and explicitly confront the issue of isolation" by creating multiple avenues of interaction among educators and promoting inquiry-oriented practices while working toward high standards of student performance (2000, 32).

Studies on school reform, including those that are focused on curriculum and instruction, make theoretical claims that point to the importance of a school's professional learning community. The tasks for implementing a new curriculum in a school can be daunting. The instructional resources themselves often do not present significant problems, but putting them to use in the classroom can pose challenges. Schools labeled as urban and low-performing and serving predominately low-income and minority students are often void of a school community grounded in relational trust (Sarason 1995; Payne 2002). This situation raises critical questions for those working for equity in education. How do school leaders bring instructional reform to the subcultures in those schools—subcultures that are set in their views about one another and their children? In other words, is the quality of a school's culture or community critical to student learning and achievement, or is the notion of a professional learning community an end in itself, only to enhance the quality of life for the teachers?

## Defining "Professional Learning Community"

The term *professional learning community* is self-defining. And this may be the reason that there is no universal definition of a professional learning community (Hord 1997). DuFour notes that currently people use the term to describe a wide range of groupings within education—a grade-level teaching team, a school committee, a high school department, an entire school district, a national professional organization, and so on. He expresses concern that the term "has been used so ubiquitously that it is in danger of losing all meaning" (2004, 6). More than two decades ago, Hord (1997) described professional learning communities as schools in which the staff as a whole consistently operates along five dimensions: (1) supportive and shared leadership; (2) shared values and vision; (3) collective learning and application of learning; (4) supportive conditions; and (5) shared personal practice. These attributes are evident in the core principles of professional learning communities that DuFour (2004) defines as the *big ideas*: (1) ensuring that students learn by shifting the focus on teaching to a focus on learning; (2) creating a culture of collaboration in which teachers are systematically involved in analyzing and improving their practice; and (3) focusing on results—having the staff take the crucial steps to confront data on student achievement and work together to improve results. Professional learning communities can provide the ways and means to address school reform.

## Establishing a Professional Learning Community

Grossman and Wineberg presented findings from an "instructive case" on a professional development project (2000, 7). The researchers posed this question: "What makes a teacher community different from a gathering of teachers?" Through a study of their own involvement as leaders and participants in the group over time and analysis of teacher interviews, evaluations, and transcripts of six whole-group discussions, they created a model of the formation of a teacher professional learning community. They identified the developmental stages as *beginning, evolving,* and *maturity.* Across these stages, several factors come into play and are transformed as the group becomes more established: (1) group identity and norms; (2) understanding differences; (3) negotiating tension; and (4) communal responsibility for personal growth (Grossman and Wineberg 2000, 45). This study illustrates how, over time, a professional learning community nourishes teachers.

Previously, I have noted that South Loop teachers had opportunities to talk with one another about formative assessment practices. In my case study, I wanted to document this process to illustrate the central role it played in fostering a collegial environment and contributing to effective teaching practices.

Professional learning communities evolved through recognition of "uncomfortable evidence" from school reform in the 1990s (Hopkins and Reynolds 2001, 460). This evidence was from national and international school reforms that were not that successful. These researchers argued that an emphasis on classroom instruction and professional capacity-building was lacking in most reforms, resulting in stagnant, flat student achievement results. To illustrate the usefulness of professional learning communities, Hopkins and Reynolds examined Chicago school reform through research conducted by the Consortium on Chicago School Research. Pointing to 1994, Hopkins and Reynolds noted that the Chicago district was reorganized, "with decentralized development being retained within a context of local capacity-building and external accountability" (2001, 462). At that time, Chicago also added five functions to its reform for schools; two of the five were focused on stimulating innovation and building capacity, which are at the core of professional learning communities. Hopkins and Reynolds maintain that findings from this research point to the importance of site-based professional learning communities, elevating this notion to the forefront of reform. They conclude that professional development is "...the focus on improving instruction within the context of the curriculum, using a methodology of collaborative inquiry into student learning, that provides the usefulness for...school improvement efforts" (2001, 468). Such professional development is best accomplished within a professional learning community. The role of a professional learning community to serve as a reform strategy soon became an accepted feature of school change efforts.

Elmore argues against the notion that improvement in schools must take a long time and must involve more money. He claims that "improvements in instruction have immediate effects on student learning wherever they occur, and these effects are usually demonstrable through skillful assessment and observation of students' work" (2002, 31). Professional development, Elmore claims, should be at the core of school and district improvement aimed at increasing student achievement. To be effective, professional development must be tied to a structure or system of improvement and be a quality experience for the school and district. I knew that a quality experience was essential for South Loop teachers if they were to join in the efforts to improve conditions at the school—conditions that affected the entire community. How that quality experience was achieved is the story told in this book.

## Perceptions of Professional Learning Communities

Research on the perceptions of professional learning communities provides evidence that it is critical for the school community to engage in dialogue focused on school improvement and student achievement (Huffman and Jacobsen 2003). Through their research, Hoffman and Jacobsen identified key qualities of professional learning communities: a safe environment to share strategies, beliefs, and practices; a democratic organization guided by ethics and positive values; and collaborative or transformational leadership.

Professional learning communities have the potential to effect significant changes in school conditions. Fullan, Hill, and Crévola focus on the role of professional learning communities in building the capacity of school systems to change. They contend that professional learning groups function "principally through a combination of demonstration teaching, mentoring, coaching, and opportunities for the team to debrief and reflect on teachers' practice and progress" (2006, 94). These observations are consistent with the current trend towards school-based, embedded professional development. However, Cohen and Hill (2001) caution that professional learning communities can be inadvertently counterproductive if their interactions reinforce ineffective teaching practices. One way to ensure that this does not happen is to design policies that address deliberate practices for improvement. The process we followed at South Loop is evidence of this advice: formative assessments linked to learning outcomes helped teachers to make informed decisions about instruction, new resources for reading and math brought coherence to the curriculum across the grades and structures (e.g., grade-level team meetings, literacy coaches) enabled teachers to work collaboratively. The venue for teacher learning and development must provide allowances for applying, experimenting, and sharing assessment experiences with colleagues (Schmoker 2004).

Exploring the notion of the sustainability of learning communities in innovative schools, Giles and Hargreaves (2006) conducted a case study of three such schools. This research sought to determine if it is possible to sustain success over time while in the midst of changing school and district demands and expectations. Although the results of the study are not generalizable, this research suggests that professional learning communities can counteract many forces that can eat away at the core elements and structures of the community. The authors note that while current reform movements are championing the development of professional learning communities, prescriptive standardized reform movements consume the time and energy of teachers, eating away at their learning community. While these claims are of value to the debate on standards-based reforms, it is necessary to acknowledge that these reforms are implemented in a variety of different ways in states, districts, and schools.

McLaughlin and Talbert present compelling evidence that school-based teacher learning communities are critical for continuous and improved student achievement (2003). They describe three functions that teacher learning communities serve: "build and manage knowledge; …create shared language and standards for practice and student outcomes; and sustain aspects of their school's culture vital to continued, consistent norms and instructional practice" (2003, 5). On a discouraging note, the researchers contend that even though there is "compelling evidence of their special value to teaching and learning, school-based teacher learning communities are neither common in American schools nor featured as policy responses to improving student outcomes" (2003, 113). Fortunately, such is not the case in Chicago Public Schools, where our efforts at South Loop are providing the basis for reforms in other schools. Recall from the

Introduction the decision of the Chicago Board of Education in 2008 to approve the opening of a new school based on the "South Loop way." I hope this book will bring a practical voice to helping others overcome roadblocks that they may encounter when building teacher learning communities.

Professional learning communities constantly evolve because of the social contexts in which they function. Ideally, they serve to enhance teachers' knowledge and skills through experiences that are shared in constructive relationships and conversations with others who are engaged in common work. Critical to the work at South Loop was how the teachers worked with one another and with their students. That is where the school leadership team situated the resources and support at South Loop. Of course, it was not as easy as it may sound, as there are never enough resources and too many competing demands. The title of this book, *Professional Learning Communities: Using Data in Decision Making to Improve Student Learning*, captures the essential theme of learning communities. The South Loop professional learning community developed because teachers were given the time and resources to work together, and collaboration was expected and became a part of the culture.

## Framing the Issues

Achieving change within a school is a complex process that is influenced by factors within and external to the institution—school administration, teachers, students, instructional resources, community demographics, government policy mandates, district initiatives, funding, and so on. Despite conflicting priorities that may stem from

> "The nature of relationships among the adults within a school has a greater influence on the character and quality of that school and on student accomplishment than anything else. If the relationships between administrators and teachers are trusting, generous, helpful, and cooperative, then the relationships between teachers and students, between students and students, and between teachers and parents are likely to be trusting, generous, helpful, and cooperative. If, on the other hand, relationships between administrators and teachers are fearful, competitive, suspicious, and corrosive, then these qualities will disseminate throughout the school community."
>
> —Barth (2006, 8)

these disparate factors, the singular purpose of schooling cannot be overlooked or denied—that is, improving learning opportunities for all students. Based on my experiences working in schools as a teacher and principal, I think it is safe to say that the conditions at South Loop are likely to exist to some degree in many schools in our country. The story of South Loop shows the power that teams of teachers can have on the learning community of a school—there can be great synergy. For South Loop, the whole became greater than the sum of its parts.

The five core principles that were listed at the beginning of this chapter are key to the work that took place at South Loop, work that many teachers had the courage to engage in. It took courage to acknowledge and accept the foundation that the route to improving student learning is improving classroom instruction. It took courage for teacher teams to agree that there could be other ways to address the teaching and learning needs of their students. The teachers took risks by discussing the assessments and assessment data of their students. The risks taken to develop a learning community, in supportive systems and structures, resulted in effective instructional practices designed to meet individual student learning.

## *Reflection: Thinking About Teaching and Learning*

1. From the chapter, select one quotation that best represents your perspective about the complexities of school-level change. Share your observations about the quotation with colleagues, or jot down some thoughts in your professional learning journal.

2. To what extent do you think the comments of the South Loop teacher (p. 33) and the literacy coaches (p. 46) are representative of educators with whom you have worked or are now working? How would you deal with such situations if you were participating in a program to improve teaching and learning in the school?

3. In what ways has the current emphasis on assessment, particularly high-stakes tests, affected the way you teach and the conversations you have with colleagues?

4. In your situation, which factors both within the school and outside of the school have positively contributed to school-level change? Which factors have impeded changes that you and your colleagues desired?

# Chapter 3

# *A Framework for School-Level Change*

The research and researchers reviewed in the previous chapter affirm that teacher professional learning communities are important for school development, and that the use of the standards and assessments are also essential for improvement. That said, the problem of student underachievement in reading is a familiar challenge to most urban school leaders and teachers. Finding ways to meet this challenge underlies ongoing efforts for school-level change. Information about student reading achievement across the states is available from the National Assessment of Educational Progress (NAEP). An analysis of these data shows that fourth- and eighth-grade students scored two points higher along a 500-point scale in 2005 than in the 1992 NAEP assessment for grades four and eight. Also, White, Black, and Hispanic students scored higher in 2005 than in 2003; yet the achievement gap between White and Black or Hispanic students still remains significant. Although we may feel somewhat heartened with these slight improvements in student performance, the increases are not sufficient in the context of national and global advances in science and technology over the past 30 years. NAEP reading scores have remained flat while the demand for literacy in the workplace has increased, putting the nation's students at a greater disadvantage than they were 30 years ago.

The 2005 NAEP reading achievement data show that the nation's fourth- and eighth-grade students were still at a basic or below-basic level of proficiency in reading. This finding was especially true in states with large urban districts such as Chicago's District 299 in Illinois. Figures 3.1 and 3.2 on the following page show NAEP results for fourth and eighth grades, respectively, for public schools in the city of Chicago, the state of Illinois, and nationally. (See Appendix 3.1 and 3.2 on pp. 155–158 for definitions of basic, proficient, and advanced achievement levels.) The 2005 data for Chicago Public

Schools (CPS) illustrate that a significant percentage of students were at below-basic proficiency when it came to reading proficiency.

**Figure 3.1. The Nation's Report Card 2005 Reading—Grade 4**

|  | Below-Basic | Basic | Proficient | Advanced |
|---|---|---|---|---|
| Chicago Public | 60 | 27 | 12 | 2 |
| Illinois Public | 38 | 33 | 23 | 7 |
| Large Central City Public | 56 | 27 | 14 | 3 |
| Nation Public | 38 | 33 | 23 | 7 |

Sources: National Center for Education Statistics. (2005). The Nation's Report Card: *Trial Urban District Assessment Reading 2005*; National Center for Education Statistics. (2005). The Nation's Report Card: *Reading 2005 State Snapshot Reports for Grade 4.*

**Figure 3.2. The Nation's Report Card 2005 Reading—Grade 8**

|  | Below-Basic | Basic | Proficient | Advanced |
|---|---|---|---|---|
| Chicago Public | 40 | 42 | 16 | 1 |
| Illinois Public | 25 | 44 | 28 | 3 |
| Large Central City Public | 40 | 40 | 18 | 1 |
| Nation Public | 27 | 42 | 26 | 3 |

Sources: National Center for Education Statistics. (2005). The Nation's Report Card: *Trial Urban District Assessment Reading 2005*; National Center for Education Statistics. (2005). The Nation's Report Card: *Reading 2005 State Snapshot Reports for Grade 8.*

Districtwide data for CPS from the 2005 Illinois State Report Card show results similar to the NAEP results. These data, shown in Figure 3.3, illustrate that 55.4% of the district's students scored below state standards on the Illinois Standards Achievement Test (ISAT), which is designed to measure individual student achievement on the Illinois State Learning Standards.

**Figure 3.3. 2005 Illinois State Report Card**

|  | Percentage of Students Meeting or Exceeding the Standards |
|---|---|
| Chicago Public | 44.6 |
| Illinois Public | 65.2 |

Source: The State Board of Education eReport Card Public Site.

## Chicago's Efforts to Improve Reading Achievement

Data for Chicago's District 299 reveal a chronic condition in reading achievement among the city's youth. These data are among many indicators frustrating a district focused on school reform since 1988. In that year, CPS instituted radical policies shifting governance from central to local control and then, in 1995, to a shared power structure between the city's mayor, the board of education, and local school councils. Along with policies addressing issues of governance, the district instituted mandates calling for increased student achievement and holding school personnel accountable for such efforts. These mandates resulted in increased administrative and structural stability for the school system, but only mild gains in student achievement.

In 2001, with the goal of increasing academic achievement, Mayor Richard M. Daley focused the attention of the district on reading. His efforts resulted in the formation of an expert panel on reading instruction and a daylong forum that brought together key district personnel and citywide educational leaders to discuss possible solutions to low achievement in reading. Mayor Daley and his advisors defined the problem and worked with key constituencies to develop a plan to address lagging reading scores. Soon, this led to the formation of the Chicago Reading Initiative, a broad-based initiative directed at increasing reading test scores and literacy rates of Chicago's students. In the fall of 2001, the Chicago Reading Initiative's implementation began with a two-year plan to address reading instruction in low-performing city schools. At the core of the initiative, schools were required to provide two hours of reading instruction per day, using research-based instructional strategies. The program's reading instructional framework directed the focus on the skills of word knowledge, comprehension, fluency, and writing. Other core areas were training teachers and principals, monitoring implementation, and providing instructional materials. The program also aimed at developing high-quality reading instruction and increasing student achievement in reading on standardized tests. CPS provided reading specialists to 114 schools with the lowest reading scores in the district. CPS also provided training and ongoing coaching support to those reading specialists. In addition to providing a similar description about the Chicago Reading Initiative on its website, the CPS Office of Literacy also emphasizes integrating reading instruction in all content areas. As previously noted, the primary focus of this initiative is to build teacher and school capacity in reading. CPS provided support and monitored the implementation of the initiative. Accountability measures for this implementation and defined student learning outcomes were not part of the design, as state standards were to guide the level of rigor for reading instruction. The existing standardized tests and district criteria for student promotion and school probation were the accountability measures in place to hold schools accountable for academic progress. In a decentralized system where each school is site-based managed, implementing and assessing district mandates and policy can be difficult.

> "There are two broad streams of data use, one a carrot, one a stick. The same data—attendance, demographics, test scores, teacher characteristics, school spending, course-taking patterns—can be used for diagnosis or accountability purposes or both. For example, disaggregating test scores by identifiable groups of youngsters can provide the key to either bettering instruction or finger-pointing (or both)."
> —Doyle (2002, 31)

After initiating school change through several district reforms, policies, and initiatives since 1988, a significant number of urban students schooled in over 500 elementary schools in District 299 continued to perform at a level that is below-basic in reading as measured by national standardized tests (see Figures 3.1 and 3.2).

## Recognizing a Need

South Loop Elementary School was among the 500 elementary schools in District 299 where student reading achievement needed attention. The achievement at this school was below that of District 299 and Illinois State. Aware that student achievement was a significant concern at this school, I was familiar with the objectives of the Chicago Reading Initiative and knew that it would be critical to implement it when I became principal at South Loop in August 2002. As noted in the two previous chapters, the challenges that South Loop administration and teachers faced were significant. Historically, over 65% of South Loop's students in grades three through eight demonstrated below-proficiency performance on the State Board of Education's Illinois Standardized Achievement Test. Declining enrollment and school segregation were additional challenges.

The instability of the school's administration and staff were other factors affecting the school's ability to address problems with student achievement. Some of the persistent conditions at the school included high teacher autonomy, serious student discipline problems requiring frequent 911 calls to the Chicago Police Department, and the readiness of some neighbors to call the police to provide a show of force even when there were no serious disciplinary infractions. The procedures and routines for student misbehavior that were in place resulted in a line of students who had allegedly misbehaved standing in front of the administrative offices for most of the day so that they could be processed. In most cases, this led to suspension from school, or at least to calls to parents, and sometimes to the police. As a result of academic underachievement, poor grades, poor attendance (sometimes the result of student suspensions resulting from significant misconduct), or low standardized test scores, the majority of students in the promotion grades—three, six, and eight—were required to attend summer school as a last-ditch effort to move to the next grade. The need for school-level change was obvious. To be effective, any actions directed towards change would have to involve all the stakeholders—administration, teachers, students, and the community.

> "If you truly want to understand something, try to change it."
> —Lewin (n.d.)

## Building a Leadership Team

Taking a structural and systematic approach to these challenges, I wanted to develop partnerships and decide on programs to support the needs at the school. First, I sought out advice from two or three teachers as I thought through administrative decisions. It is important to note that while I met with many teachers, parents, and members of the community about their hopes for the school, I did not know any of the teachers at the school when I started. Consequently, it was difficult to gauge who was interested in working to make improvements and who wanted to keep things the same. Initially, I did not form a leadership team because (as I explained in Chapter 1) I was an interim principal for the first three months of the school year. During this time, I was engaged in the process of interviewing to serve as the school's contract principal. With the uncertainty in my tenure at the school, I thought it would be best not to begin building a leadership structure for the school until the decision was made about who would be selected to serve as the contract principal. That said, I informally reached out to a few people for advice as I made decisions and plans. These individuals were the literacy coach, two classroom teachers, a senior-level leader from the district, the director of an Urban School Leadership program at University of Illinois at Chicago, and a few parents from the Local School Council. I also had tremendous support from a fellow educator and at home from my spouse. A few months later in December, after I was selected as the contract principal for the school, I decided to set up a formal leadership team. I asked teachers to apply to serve on the team and set it up so that the composition of the team would be representative of the teachers at the school. Teachers on the team would represent those in pre-K through second grade, third grade through fifth grade, and sixth grade through eighth grade. In addition, I asked that a teacher represent the resource teachers as well as the music, library, art, and gym teachers. To facilitate this process, I asked teachers to meet in grade bands and to nominate and elect a teacher to represent them. At this time, the only criteria established for individuals to serve on the team was a commitment to work in teams on agreed-upon projects and to attend scheduled meetings. I was excited to begin working with teachers who were elected by their peers. I also added the literacy coaches to the team and, after I hired an assistant principal in February, asked that person to be part of the team.

The two main areas of focus for this group were reading instruction and the school's culture and climate. On an ongoing basis, I monitored teacher follow-through on commitments and attendance at team meetings and met individually with members of the leadership team on their involvement. In April of that year, I set out specific criteria for those who chose to volunteer to serve on the leadership team. These criteria were relatively general, but a demonstrated commitment to serve as a member of the team was critical. Leadership team members were expected to have regular attendance at meetings and to assume duties and responsibilities that led and supported either the development of the school's culture or reading instruction. Teachers were asked to complete an application and submit it to me. Making sure that I selected teachers who were representative of their peers, I selected individuals to serve on the team who demonstrated the criteria established over the first eight months of the school year.

## Decisions and a Decision-Making Process

As previously stated, during the first part of the year I consulted on an individual basis with a few people. These contacts provided me a context that enabled me to better understand the depth of the issues and concerns that I was experiencing at the school: the quality of teaching and learning and the quality of the school's environment— the culture and climate for students, teachers and parents, and relations between the school and its neighboring community. Through these contacts, I developed strong relationships with the various constituents as we worked together to find solutions.

This background helped me as I sought to identify resources within the school, district, and city of Chicago that could support school change. By October, the school received funding to hire a reading coach to support reading instruction. In addition, we were able to secure a university partnership with the College of Education at the University of Illinois at Chicago (UIC). At the time, UIC was working with the district to support reading instruction for 10 schools using a Standards-Based Change Process. This project was the result of a generous grant to the district from the Chicago Community Trust, a philanthropic organization that supports a variety of education- and health-related needs in the Chicago region. UIC's Partnership READ was developed to augment the district's work with the Chicago Reading Initiative by supporting a standards-based approach to reading instruction. This university partnership resulted in partial support for an additional teacher from the school who would receive training to become a literacy coach, as well as professional development support for the teachers at the school.

## Getting Faculty Buy-In

I made the case for the partnership with various stakeholders and sought support from the teachers in an attempt to gain their buy-in and willingness to participate in the activities. Within the first two months of the 2002–2003 school year, I proposed this new university partnership that would support the needs of the school, invited the teachers' participation, and gained their support to engage with Partnership READ.

"I suppose that leadership at one time meant muscle; but today it means getting along with other people."
—Ghandi (n.d.)

The principles of the Standards-Based Change Process (see Figure 2.1, p. 36) provided the guidance that was instrumental in helping the leadership team and teachers come to an agreement about making changes to improve student reading achievement. Recognizing a need is the first step in this process. South Loop teachers were well aware of the problems within the school and the community, but many felt that the possibilities for change were slim. A second critical step was organizing for change. This step involved a core group of individuals who could work collegially to establish strategies to bring about needed changes. Having colleagues take responsibility for defining the need and inviting others to participate in activities to rectify the problems were significant factors that fostered the teachers' willingness to become engaged in the change process. As the different phases of the Standards-Based Change Process illustrate, this process took time and required revisions as this team was established. As the principal, I had to make the necessary accommodations to ensure that the teacher participation would be meaningful, supported, and sustained.

## Restructuring the School Schedule

Time is one of the more pressing issues facing teachers involved in reform efforts. There never seems to be enough time to do all the things required of them—plan lessons, observe and interpret student learning, cope with unexpected situations, deal with discipline issues, handle parental inquiries, focus on accountability demands of high-stakes assessment, and participate in professional development activities. The gift of time is something that appeals to all teachers. Certainly, teachers at South Loop needed time to get together if anything was to be accomplished in raising student achievement. This time had to be found within the schedule of the school day.

By January of 2003, I made the decision to increase the time available for teacher professional development by instituting a restructured school day schedule. This new schedule had two elements: (1) an extra 90 minutes of professional development time was scheduled every 15 school days, and (2) grade-level meetings were held during the school day where teachers met on a weekly basis for 40 minutes with others who taught in the same grade level. The idea of regularly scheduled time for professional development or grade-level meetings was new to the teachers. You may recall the comments of two literacy coaches whose reflections about collaboration prior to the 2003 school year are quoted in Chapter 2. In contrast, these same individuals recalled how time was used during some of the schoolwide professional development sessions during the 2003 school year. One workshop was on the Illinois Learning Standards.

**Literacy Coach 2:** *I want to say it was around January. That was the first time we were introduced to the element of learning standards. The first time I ever saw that.*

**Literacy Coach 1:** *Right. Where someone actually took the time to explain the standards and what a benchmark was, and you know [what it is].*

**Literacy Coach 2:** *Like, we did not use them at all…when we were introduced to it, it was in the gym here at the school. It was like a workshop PD.*

## Taking Action to Address Needs

By the spring of the same year, as a result of meeting for 60–90 minutes every week, the school's leadership team established clear school-improvement priorities and goals. As previously noted, both the school's culture and student academic achievement were in need of improvement. Administrators and some teachers agreed to work together to guide the change that was taking place. To accomplish this, some of the members of the school's leadership team focused on school culture and climate, while other members of the team led change in curriculum and instruction, with an initial focus on reading. The strength in this approach is that there was a core school leadership team, and two subcommittees or teams that focused on the core initiatives. The leaders of these committees provided reports to the leadership team, and the leadership team provided support for the committees. These structures and routines provided a consistent group of school leaders with current information on which to base decisions as they worked together toward needed changes. This foundation provided continuity and coherence for the work that was taking place at the school. The committees and leadership team met throughout the spring and summer of 2003 to gear up for the start of the 2004 school year.

> "People underestimate their capacity for change. There is never a right time to do a difficult thing. A leader's job is to help people have a vision of their potential"
>
> —Porter (n.d.)

The curriculum and instruction committee, led by the literacy coaches, used the Standards-Based Change framework and support provided by UIC's Partnership READ. Descriptions of how the school implemented this work are provided in the chapters that follow. The work of the committee that was core to supporting school change in culture and climate is the topic for another study, so it is not dealt with in this book. It is important to note that a change in the school's climate and culture needed to happen for South Loop, and that its change was critical to the success of the school. Recognizing that changing the culture at South Loop was of utmost importance, I researched the availability of programs that could provide assistance in this area. Funding from the district grant I applied for made it easy to choose a program from those available. This grant supported the school in establishing schoolwide systems, structures, and routines that would clearly define expectations for behavior and communications at SLES. With funding available, the culture and climate committee was able to begin its work in earnest. This grant provided resources to implement Positive Behavioral Interventions and Supports (PBIS), a system that provides a framework and process that districts and schools can use to develop and establish schoolwide systems, structures, and routines. The funding provided a coach to support program implementation one day per week at South Loop. Additional support was in the form of professional development for teachers and staff, along with coaching to enable implementation of PBIS. The coach also worked with the committee on school culture. Once a district or school decides to implement this program, PBIS training using the train-the-trainer model is provided. South Loop first sent a team of teachers and administrators to a three-day workshop to learn about implementation strategies and to determine roles for each member of the team. Once trained, the PBIS coach and school-based team led the implementation at South Loop. It was also critical for the school administration to integrate all aspects of the implementation into school handbooks, policies, and procedures. In order to achieve change through PBIS, the systems and structures that would be developed must become expectations for everyone at the school. (For more information about this system, refer to the PBIS website at **http://www.pbis.org/main.htm**.)

The first activity at the school was to define three core values for the school and then define what that would look like on the playground, in the hallway, on a field trip, in the library, in the lunchroom, in the washroom, and so on. The core values determined and agreed upon by the school became what is now known as "The South Loop Way: Be Safe, Be Responsible, Be Respectful." Once the school defined what it would look like to be safe, responsible, and respectful in each area of the school, the adults then needed to develop language to communicate the expectations. For example, if it was decided that walking in the halls, rather than running, was necessary for safety, then teachers must model, teach, and reteach the appropriate behavior when it is not happening. Also, when correcting students, the adults in the school were to say what they expected, not emphasize what the student was doing. For example, if a student were running down the hall, the adult would say, "Walk!" not, "Stop running!" These were subtle, yet important differences. This approach required significant adult learning and coaching as we worked to change our culture, which meant we were working to change our choices, actions, and words, as well as ourselves.

"Slowly, by turning from what we learn with others to what we learn alone, we begin to have a sense of the speed of our learning, the first few chapters of our own eccentric life story. Where do we practice it? Where may our story happen best? When we leave the lively hive of this school, what larger hive do we seek?"
—Stafford (n.d.)

The school's literacy coach played a critical role in moving forward to implement the work of the committee on curriculum and instruction. Working closely with the committee members, UIC's Partnership READ, and the principal, the coach guided development of the school's approach to increasing student achievement. Specifically, key areas of responsibility for the coach included leading grade-level teams and grade-level team meetings, developing and conducting professional development workshops, and working with teacher teams on a variety of tasks related to curriculum and instruction. UIC's Partnership READ and the school leadership team, which included the literacy coach, played an essential role in determining the agenda and finding the support for site-based professional development.

## Acquiring Additional Funds

With the support of the Local School Council, the school's budget, and funding from grants, the leadership team decided to purchase new reading and math series for all the pre-K through eighth-grade students for the upcoming school year. Over the years to come, the principal and a small but committed team of parent volunteers, knowing the limits of school funding, developed ways for the parents and the community to support the priorities and goals of the school, both financially and through direct service. One example was the creation of a nonprofit organization, The Family and Friends of South Loop, an organization specifically designed to oversee fund-raising activities to support the needs of the school.

The leadership team also addressed the pressing need for change in its school culture. Working on the assumption that more time was needed during the day with the students and that students needed a safe place to be after school and over the summer, the administration developed a model for funding and support for a summer camp and an after-school program. This resource provided a safe learning environment for all students until at least 6:00 p.m. each day and throughout the summer.

## Clarifying Expectations for Teachers

Supports and processes to manage human resources were also critical considerations. These issues were addressed in a variety of ways. The leadership team developed a draft of local criteria that would become part of teacher evaluation for the 2004 school year, and I presented it to the teachers in the spring of 2003. Although Chicago Public Schools has a generic teacher evaluation form, schools can opt to develop and present

> "Effective teachers constitute a valuable human resource for schools—one that needs to be treasured and supported. ...keeping good teachers—both novices and veterans—requires attention to working conditions that matter to teachers. ...key conditions include teacher participation in decision making, strong and supportive instructional leadership from principals, and collegial learning opportunities."
> —Darling-Hammond (2003, 7, 13)

additional criteria to use in evaluating teachers. The leadership team wanted teachers to know what would be expected of them for the upcoming school year. These criteria include guidelines for curriculum planning and implementation, as well as guidelines for engaging in professional development and other collegial activities, communicating with parents, and participating in community-related events. The complete document is provided in Appendix 3.3 (pp. 159–160).

Staff turnover often occurs when some teachers choose to leave at the end of each school year, and this was the case at South Loop. In interviews with prospective teachers, I wanted to know about their commitment to the initiatives and the change that was taking place at the school, in addition to their professional qualifications and experience. The school leadership also developed relationships with local colleges and schools of education. Through these relationships, student teachers were awarded full-year placements and paired with mentor teachers. Along with significant experience and exposure, these student teachers provided a pool of possible candidates for the following year. Their presence in the school also helped meet students' learning needs by increasing the number of adults available to help with instruction. From the university perspective, these placements were opportunities for student teachers to work and learn in a challenging urban environment in a school that was committed to improving teaching and learning.

## One Year of Change at South Loop

The school leadership brought 14 primary inputs to the school over the course of one year, August 2002 through August 2003. Starting with a new administration, the efforts at reform continued to evolve with the creation of faculty leadership teams, the development of partnerships with local universities, implementation of Standards-Based Change Process, the provision of opportunities for ongoing professional learning, and the building of parent and community partnerships. The scope of these activities is shown in Figure 3.4 on the following page.

**Figure 3.4. Activities for Change at South Loop: August 2002–August 2003**

| August–December 2002 | January–March 2003 | April–May 2003 | June–August 2003 |
|---|---|---|---|
| • New Administration<br><br>• University Partnership: Standards-Based Change Process<br><br>• Literacy Coaches | • Grade-Level Team Meetings<br><br>• Restructured School Day<br><br>• Optional Teacher Workshops—After School<br><br>• Leadership Teams | • PBIS<br><br>• Parent and Community Partnerships<br><br>• Coherent Reading and Math Materials<br><br>• Human Resource Management<br><br>• Teacher Evaluation: Local Criteria | • Summer Work: Leadership Teams<br><br>• Extended Learning Programs<br><br>• University Partnerships: Student Teachers<br><br>• Implement and Further Develop the Reform Strategy |

Once implemented, these supports were nurtured and developed over the next four years. Was this too much change at once? Would students benefit from the hard work and commitment of many teachers, parents, and administrators? These and many more questions concerned administrators and the leadership teams as they forged plans for implementation. The hope and belief was that it would benefit students. In the next chapters, we will look at what actually occurred in the years 2004 through 2007.

## Reflection: Thinking About Teaching and Learning

1. From the chapter, select one quotation that best represents your perspective about conditions that favor school-level change. Share your observations about the quotation with colleagues, or jot down some thoughts in your professional learning journal.

2. What evidence do you and your colleagues draw upon to determine where changes are needed in the school—changes in instructional practices, changes in collegial communication, and changes in the culture of the school?

3. Faculty "buy-in" and faculty "push-back" are powerful elements that can determine the success or failure of change efforts within a school. Describe your experiences with both situations. What conditions favor faculty "buy-in"? What conditions produce faculty "push-back"?

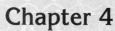

## Chapter 4

# *Actions Leading to Change*

Teachers' professional knowledge is closely linked to the outcomes that they expect for their students. As described in Chapter 3, several steps were necessary to establish an environment at South Loop Elementary School in which the administration, teachers, and coaches moved towards mutual acceptance of actions that could be taken to improve student achievement. We had to become sufficiently comfortable with one another to have open conversations about pressing questions related to student achievement: What data were available to teachers? How were these data collected? Did everyone follow the same routines for collecting data? How did teachers use the results to guide instruction? What changes in student achievement were we hoping to accomplish?

The purchase of new instructional materials for reading and math set the stage for achieving curriculum consistency, a factor that was noticeably absent when the school lacked coherence with the resources, and teachers made individual decisions about curriculum and materials. Consequently, the approach to instruction was comparatively nonsystematic and incoherent. Lack of curriculum consistency is characteristic of schools where teacher isolation is an accepted part of the culture. "Just leave me alone and let me teach!" is a familiar plea in such schools, notably at times when efforts are underway to change instructional practices and the culture of the school. Teachers at South Loop had faced administrative instability, as well as issues surrounding student behavior and community controversies, and it was not surprising that some of them preferred to work in isolation. One teacher described the situation in this way:

**Teacher:** *Everybody went in their room and did their own thing; there was not a lot of consistency across grade levels or even among grade levels. If you taught next door to a fourth grade teacher, she was using different books than you were using. We had all kinds of series left over from years. You might have a favorite reading series that you had found or picked up over the years and somebody else was using a different one.*

Isolation is the enemy of improvement. Haycock's findings are evidence of this problem: if we leave virtually every instructional choice up to individual teachers who work alone, then inferior practices will dominate in most schools (2005).

"The traditional school often functions as a collection of independent contractors united by a common parking lot."
—Eaker as cited in Schmoker (2006, 23)

From 2003 through 2007, participation in various stages of the Standards-Based Change Process enabled the leadership team, literacy coaches, and teachers to make changes that produced improvements in student reading achievement. These actions included developing formative assessments and organizing grade-level team meetings where teachers had opportunities to engage in discussions about teaching and learning. In addition to leading to improved student achievement, these activities revealed changes in the culture at South Loop.

## Developing Formative Assessments

In order to develop a formative assessment, it was necessary for the teachers to develop a standards-based learning outcome for their grade levels, develop an assessment that reflected the level of rigor expected to meet the demands of the outcome, and determine a way to score student performance on that assessment. Since the school was just beginning to learn about a standards-based approach to teaching and learning, the formative assessments narrowly focused on key tasks and proficiencies for reading comprehension and writing. The reading comprehension assessment required students to read a grade-appropriate passage, respond to 10 multiple-choice questions, and respond in writing to a prompt based on the selection. In the writing assessment, students responded to a writing prompt. The teachers scored the assessments using a rubric to generate data and analyzed the data to determine what the results revealed about student instructional needs.

## Reading Comprehension Assessments and Results in the 2005 School Year

The documents that follow show examples of reading comprehension and writing outcomes, summaries of student achievement data on the selected outcome over the course of the 2005 school year, and a scoring rubric for writing. Grounded in the state's learning standards, these outcomes and rubrics were the foundation for the development of formative assessments. Figure 4.1 on the following page is an example of a third-grade comprehension outcome. At the top of this figure is an outcome statement. This statement was designed to focus teaching and learning by providing an outcome that represented six main learning benchmarks. These reading comprehension tasks reflect the state standards that students are expected to meet by the end of the year for their grade levels. The outcome statement was used to help students understand what they were expected to learn. For example, the outcome statement can be rephrased as, "I can tell the difference between fiction and nonfiction books, tell what is important in a text, make inferences, and summarize what I've read."

**Figure 4.1. Standards-Based Reading Comprehension Learning Outcome, Third Grade, South Loop Elementary School, 2005**

---

### Third Grade Comprehension Outcome

Students will be able to identify literary works, demonstrate informational sources, recall explicit ideas and contruct inferences.

Benchmarks: 2.A.2b, 2.A.2c, 1.B.2a, 1.B.2b, 1.C.2d, 2.A.2b

- Connect ideas/experiences with that of the author
- Explain the main ideas
- Explain important facts from the text
- Use examples and details to support the answer
- Discuss author's ideas
- Discuss personal ideas

---

The next two figures illustrate how teachers aggregated student achievement data on formative assessments administered in September, January, and May. Figure 4.2 on the following page shows the number of students who were working on, meeting, or exceeding the outcome as assessed. The assessment consisted of 10 multiple-choice questions developed by teachers and modeled on sample assessments from the Illinois Standards Achievement Test. For example, of the 10 questions for this assessment, one question assessed literary works, three questions assessed inference, four questions assessed explicit ideas, and two questions assessed word knowledge.

The sample assessments were readily available on the website of the Illinois State Board of Education. The assessment results show progress over the course of the school year. In September, all the students in one third-grade class were working on the outcome. The January assessment data, for that same classroom, report that four students were meeting the outcome and the rest of the students were working on it. By the end of the school year, the classroom data showed that six students were working on the outcome, 11 were meeting the outcome, and four were exceeding it.

**Figure 4.2. Comprehension Multiple Choice Student Achievement Data, Third Grade Class, South Loop Elementary School, 2005**

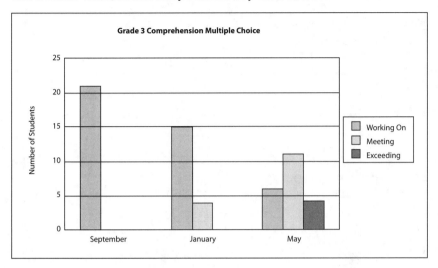

In addition to teacher-developed multiple choice assessments, the school also developed a written assessment to provide another data set to help determine the level of proficiency for students' reading comprehension. Modeled on sample assessments of the Illinois State Achievement Test, this assessment took into consideration additional higher-level tasks or proficiencies that students needed to demonstrate. Once the students completed the assessments, teachers scored student responses using a rubric. Teachers aggregated data from the assessment and reported data from their classes over the course of a school year, as illustrated in Figure 4.3 on the following page. In September, two students were meeting the outcome and 19 were working on it. In January, 11 were working on the outcome, and seven students were meeting the outcome. By May, nine students were working on the outcome, four were meeting it, and five were exceeding the outcome. While the goal was to move all students to the Meeting and Exceeding categories, this process was still relatively new to the school, and we were working to develop strong instructional practices for all students in all grades.

**Figure 4.3. Comprehension Extended Response Student Achievement Data, Third Grade Class, South Loop Elementary School, 2005**

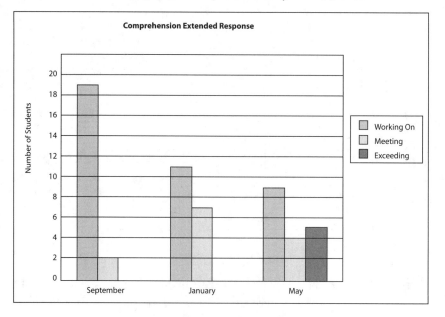

*Writing Assessments and Results in the 2005 School Year*

We developed writing assessments based on the learning outcomes for students following the approach described for reading comprehension. Figure 4.4 on the following page shows the third-grade writing outcome. The outcome statement is at the top of the figure. Designed to focus on teaching and learning, the outcome represented six main learning benchmarks. In addition to the outcome statement, the document highlights 13 of the main writing tasks that the state standards expect students to demonstrate by the end of the year for their grade levels. Like the reading comprehension outcome, this outcome was also expressed so that students could understand what was critical for them to accomplish, as illustrated in the "I can" statement: "I can organize my thoughts and write multiple paragraphs that focus on a topic and include voice and supporting details."

**Figure 4.4. Standards-Based Writing Learning Outcome, Third Grade, South Loop Elementary School, 2005**

---

## Third-Grade Writing Outcome

Students will demonstrate focus, organization, correct use of conventions, elaboration/support, and integration when writing for a variety of purposes.

Benchmarks 3.A.2, 3.B.2a, 3.B.2b, 3.B.2c, 3.B.2d, 3.C.2a

- Topic introduced clearly
- Stays on topic all the time and makes sense
- Closing relates to the topic
- Details and examples used to explain
- Word choice is interesting
- Paper has a plan
- Transitions are used appropriately
- Sentences do not all start the same
- Complete sentences used
- Punctuation and capitalization used correctly
- Indentation used correctly
- Some errors, but reader understands writing
- Paper fully developed

---

A rubric was used to score student writing. Figure 4.5 on the following pages is an example of a rubric that was used to score the work the students did on a third-grade writing assessment. This rubric was developed by modifying rubrics available on the Illinois State Board of Education website. This rubric includes a six-point scale for focus, elaboration, organization, and integration (double score), and a two-point scale for conventions.

**Figure 4.5. Standards-Based Rubric for Scoring Writing Assessments, Third Grade, South Loop Elementary School, 2005**

|   | Focus | Elaboration |
|---|-------|-------------|
| 6 | I introduced my topic clearly. My paper stays on topic all the time, and it makes sense. The closing relates to the topic. If I previewed, I wrote about each point mentioned in the preview. | I used many details and examples to explain. My word choice is interesting. |
| 5 | I introduced my subject or position. I kept my paper focused at all times, and my ideas make sense. If I previewed, I wrote about each point mentioned in the preview. | I used some details and examples to explain my subject or position. |
| 4 | The subject may not be clear to the reader. The paper sometimes drifts from the subject, and the paper sometimes doesn't make sense. There may not be a closing. Not every point that was previewed is explained in the paper. | My paper has few details and few examples as part of the explanation. Details may look like a list. |
| 3 | The subject is not very clear. I wrote about many ideas with more than one subject. I may not have written enough. My paper may not be persuasive or expository. | I did not explain my ideas. Details are a list. I may not have written enough. |
| 2 | The subject of my paper is not clear. Ideas in the paper do not seem to go together. I may not have written enough. | I tried to write details. My details were unclear. I may not have written enough. |
| 1 | The paper has no topic. I did not write enough. | I did not include details. I did not write enough. |
| | Conventions | |
| 2 | I used complete sentences. I spelled most common words correctly. I used capitalization and punctuation correctly. I have some major errors, but readers can still understand my writing. | |

**Figure 4.5. Standards-Based Rubric for Scoring Writing Assessments, Third Grade, South Loop Elementary School, 2005** *(cont.)*

| | Organization | Integration (double score) |
|---|---|---|
| 6 | My paper has a plan.<br>Paragraphs are connected, and all the transitions are appropriate.<br>The sentences do not all start the same. | My paper is fully developed and is outstanding in all areas. |
| 5 | My paper has a plan.<br>My paper is connected between paragraphs, and most transitions are appropriate.<br>A few ideas don't fit the plan. | My paper has everything it needs, but there is room for improvement. |
| 4 | My paper has a plan, but it may not be clear to my readers.<br>My paper has some connections between paragraphs, but not all of them are appropriate.<br>Some ideas don't fit the plan of the paper. | My paper is simple, but it includes the basics. |
| 3 | The plan of my paper is not clear.<br>My paper has transitions that do not make sense.<br>Many ideas do not fit the plan. I did not write a persuasive or expository paper.<br>I may not have written enough. | My paper is partially developed with small parts not developed completely. |
| 2 | The plan of my paper is confusing.<br>I may not have written enough. | My ideas are confusing to my readers because big parts are missing.<br>I may not have written enough. |
| 1 | The paper is very confusing.<br>I did not write enough. | I did not follow the directions.<br>I did not write enough. |
| | Conventions | |
| 1 | I have many major errors.<br>I have so many errors that readers cannot understand my writing. | |

| Working on the Standard | Meeting the Standard | Exceeding the Standard |
|---|---|---|
| 21 or less | 22–29 | 30–32 |

Developed by South Loop Elementary School and adapted from the Illinois State Board of Education

Figure 4.6 shows student achievement data from the writing assessments administered over the course of a school year. For the first assessment, 19 students were working on the tasks outlined in the writing outcome and two students were meeting these expectations. In January, 13 students were working on meeting the outcome and seven students were meeting the writing outcome. By May, seven students were working in the outcome, seven students were meeting the outcome, and three students were exceeding the outcome in writing.

**Figure 4.6. Writing Student Achievement Data, Third Grade Class, South Loop Elementary School, 2005**

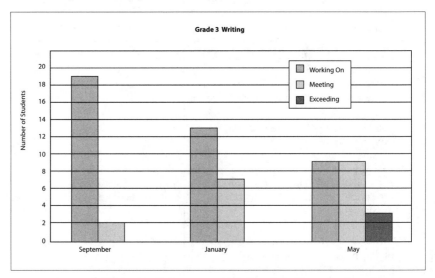

Creating and scoring formative assessments provided a common focus for the school leadership, teachers, and literacy coaches to work on together. Such efforts were helpful in addressing the issue of teacher isolation. More significantly, such activities provided opportunities for teachers to become participants and contributors rather than passive bystanders. Furthermore, teachers now had access to data showing student achievement related to the standards—they were able to witness the benefits of standards-based instruction and ongoing formative assessment.

## South Loop Achievement Data from the Illinois State Achievement Test

In the previous section, I have provided evidence of student achievement growth based on teacher-developed formative assessments linked to learning outcomes. However, student achievement was also measured on the Illinois State Achievement Test (ISAT). The ISAT is used by the Illinois State Board of Education for district and school accountability for students in grades three through eight. The test is administered in March for the Chicago Public Schools (CPS), and there are clear guidelines for test administration. Test results are available to schools over the summer, typically in July or August. Data are analyzed at the state and district for any possible test effects, and the results, once they are deemed credible, are released to the public in individual school and district report cards. The school and district report cards also contain student demographic information, broken down by racial and economic subgroups.

> "The main goal of formative assessment is to inform teachers of the active knowledge, skills, and strategies their students have mastered and to point to instruction that will move students farther along the path to learning. Yet the process of translating assessment into instructional decision making is far from easy."
>
> —Buhle and Blachowicz (2009, 42)

Data were acquired from the ISBE School Report Card and from the CPS for South Loop, 2003–2007. These data provide evidence of change that occurred over time in student attendance, ISAT composite and reading scores, and student demographic data (race, socioeconomic status, mobility, and student retention rate). Changes in the academic achievement and in school demographics, while not the focus of my case study, required some analysis to determine the extent to which changing demographics played in the increased student achievement.

Over the period from 2003–2007, as previously explained in Chapter 3, student achievement data illustrate academic improvement on the state standardized tests. It is important to mention again that, as the school improved, middle- and upper-income families in the attendance area began to see the school as an option and enrolled their children. When new families to the school began to enroll, the majority enrolled in the Early Childhood Program, pre-K, or kindergarten. Achievement results for new students to SLES would not be measured until the end of their third-grade year, four or five years after enrollment. What effect did these new students have on the school's performance? Achievement data tell the story. Due to reporting requirements of No Child Left Behind, school districts report achievement results on different subgroups within the school, illustrating achievement over time. In addition, CPS reports comparative data about achievement results for all elementary schools in the district, schools in their geographical areas, and schools individually (to protect individual student identity, data are not reported if there are less than 10 students).

ISAT achievement results are significant for South Loop. These results are shown in four tables—Appendix 4.1, Appendix 4.2, Appendix 4.3, and Appendix 4.4. South Loop results for ISAT composite achievement from 2002–2007 are reported in Appendix 4.1 (p. 161) and summarized as follows:

- In all areas tested, the percentage of students meeting and exceeding state standards moved from 32.4% to 83.4%.

- The District results show an increase of 23 percentage points in student achievement.

- In contrast to the District, SLES results show that student achievement increased by 51 percentage points.

The table in Appendix 4.2 (p. 162) shows ISAT reading achievement test results for SLES. Reading achievement, one of the main areas of focus for the school, also improved between 2003 and 2007. A summary of results follows:

- The percentage of students meeting and exceeding standards increased from 31.8% to 81.7%.

- The school's increase (49.9 percentage points) is almost a 50-percentage-point gain.

- The number of students taking the state test increased from 107 to 219.

- By comparison, student achievement in reading across the district increased by 19.4 percentage points.

A closer look at economic subgroups is necessary in order to determine if the increase in student achievement was the result of new middle- and upper-income families who came to the school, or if other factors provide explanations for the gains. Appendix 4.3 (p. 163) presents ISAT composite achievement results based on demographics of qualification for Free and Reduced Lunch (F&RL), 2003–2007. For all areas tested, results indicate little difference between students who do and those who do not qualify for F&RL. Notably, SLES results surpass district-level results in both demographic categories. These results are summarized in Figure 4.7.

**Figure 4.7. Summary of ISAT Composite Achievement Levels, 2003–2007**

| Demographic | South Loop Elementary School | District |
|---|---|---|
| No Free & Reduced Lunch | Achievement gain of 47.6 percentage points | Achievement gain of 23.2 percentage points |
| Free & Reduced Lunch | Achievement gain of 42.8 percentage points Only 4.8 points less than students outside the category | Achievement gain of 21.4 percentage points |

Reading achievement data related to demographic factors (2003–2007) are shown in Appendix 4.4 (p. 164). South Loop reading achievement results show greater improvement than comparable results at the district. While reading achievement gains show improvement for all students, students qualifying for F&RL showed a greater gain than students not qualifying for F&RL by 8.8 percentage points. Figure 4.8 on the following page presents a summary of these reading achievement results.

**Figure 4.8. Summary of ISAT Reading Achievement Results, Demographics: South Loop Elementary School and District 2003–2007**

| Demographic | South Loop Elementary School | District |
|---|---|---|
| No Free & Reduced Lunch | Achievement gain of 38.1 percentage points | Achievement gain of 22.3 percentage points |
| Free & Reduced Lunch | Achievement gain of 46.9 percentage points Attained 8.8 percentage point gain higher than group outside the category | Achievement gain of 19.7 percentage points |

South Loop experienced many changes during the years 2003–2007. The school leadership and teachers were growing in their ability to develop standards-based assessments, to interpret the assessment results, and to use the results to shape instruction. Gains in student achievement registered on the state reading comprehension tests contributed to the teachers' sense of accomplishment and their growing store of professional knowledge about teaching and learning.

## South Loop Student Demographics from 2003–2007

Between 2003–2007, the number of students qualifying for Free and Reduced Lunch (F&RL) at South Loop decreased by seven students, from 88 to 81 students, and students not qualifying for F&RL increased by 119, from 19 to 138 students. While the number of students who do not qualify for F&RL increased, the number of students who qualify for F&RL remained almost the same throughout the five school years. As

"I am coming clean right now. I'm a practicing classroom teacher, and I love data. Data connect me to my students and their learning, push me to high levels of reflection on my practice, and spur me to engage in dialogue with colleagues, students, and parents."
— Morrison (December 2008/ January 2009)

a result, the percentage of South Loop students who qualified for subsidy declined substantially, from 90.8% in 2003 to 28.1% in 2007, yet the number of students who qualified for F&RL remained almost the same. It is also important to situate the change in student demographics at the school within the context of the changes in scores for ISAT achievement. Data show that during the years when the school made its largest increases in achievement, there was not a significant increase of students tested who did not qualify for F&RL. These student numbers fluctuate: 19 students during 2003; 10 students during 2004; and 27 students during 2005. Prior to the reform in 2001, there were 21 students tested who did not qualify for F&RL, showing that there were more nonqualifying SES students tested during 2001 than there were during 2004 when the school made its biggest increase in achievement. After the school's first wave in achievement gains were publicized and the new programs initiated during 2003 began to stabilize, the demographics of the school changed markedly, especially in newly enrolled students in the Early Childhood Program and Kindergarten.

It is clear that all students who did not qualify for F&RL, the middle-income subgroup, scored at increasingly higher rates over the years. However, further analysis on these data is necessary to determine how individual students performed over the years. While student mobility as found on the Illinois State Board of Education School Report Card decreased from 28.5%, 2003 to 12%, 2007, mobility is a factor nonetheless. One implication from these findings is that the achievement data do not reflect the same students from year to year. It does, however, reflect student achievement between 2003 and 2007 for students in similar socioeconomic subgroups. As noted, the 4.7-percentage-point difference in reading achievement between the two subgroups is not significant, yet the fact that there are similar achievement gains for both socioeconomic subgroups, and that these greatly exceed district-level gains, suggests that internal school factors played a role in improving student achievement. That teachers reported sharp improvements in program coherence provides support for that supposition (see pp. 93–95 this chapter).

## Grade-Level Team Meetings

Teacher collaboration was central to accomplishing improvements in student achievement and changes in the school climate at South Loop. As noted in Chapter 3, during the period of August 2002 through August 2003, we took several steps to ensure that teachers became engaged in activities that enabled them to act on the need to improve student achievement. Meetings among teachers for the purpose of having conversations about teaching and learning were new for the school. The first of these meetings was scheduled at the start of the new semester in January 2003. I had adjusted the school day schedule to provide time for teachers to meet. This restructuring provided an extra 90 minutes of professional development time every 15 days and 40 minutes each week for teachers to meet with colleagues who taught at the same grade level. The recollections of two teachers reveal individual responses to the grade-level meetings:

**Teacher 1:** *I remember [a reading coach] had to come to my classroom to get me for each one. I was scared and hiding at my desk.*

**Teacher 2:** *Though [grade-level meetings were] a big change for the positive…coming from what we had, we didn't really talk curriculum much.*

The sentiments of another teacher provide a sense of the general tenor of many teachers in the school:

**Teacher 3:** *I remember [Fall 2003] coming into the library and thinking, and they put a sub in your room to cover your room and you are like out of your room for two hours while we just sat listening to…all of this. And we were just overwhelmed with it, and people weren't really thinking this would come to fruition or much would happen from it probably. And then we would leave, and the next group would come in. That was the beginning of it, and it was just a major change. The whole school became more structured, and there was just a real vision for the school.*

A primary factor affecting teachers' willingness to participate in change efforts is recognition that someone has a vision for the school—a belief that the school can become a different place—and commitment to supporting the teachers in contributing to fulfillment of that vision. The first year was a transition for the teachers' involvement in the grade-level meetings. Scheduling weekly meetings was a first step. At the outset the meetings were not easy, nor were the teachers' meetings about data or assessments. Yet, these meetings were critical in providing a foundation for the work that lay ahead. The literacy coaches remembered the initial grade-level team meetings:

> **Literacy Coach 2:** *Grade-level meetings are like pretty much the core of how things happen.*
>
> **Literacy Coach 1:** *That's where all the discussion happens.*
>
> **Literacy Coach 2:** *But the first year, it was…a transition. You know, they give us [a schedule for] mandatory [meetings], but the teachers [say], Oh, I forgot, and oh, I have to make these telephone calls, and oh, I have to grade these papers.*
>
> **Literacy Coach 1:** *The priority wasn't there from the teachers.*
>
> **Literacy Coach 2:** *And again, not to be repetitive, but none of these teachers had grade-level meetings in the past.*

As trust developed among the teachers and they recognized the reality of the vision for the school, the grade-level teams came to find the meetings valuable. When reflecting on what made the difference in the focus and quality of grade-level meetings over the years, the literacy coaches shared these observations:

> **Literacy Coach 2:** *We had the resistance. Like people didn't want to give up. They saw it as their time, not the school's time. So that was like a huge block, but quite honestly, like, I think that grade-level meeting time now [2007] is more productive. The teachers understand why they're meeting. They value what they're meeting about and they value what their colleagues have to say. That was not there five years ago. We did not have the respect of each other.*

**Literacy Coach 1:** *Right.*

**Literacy Coach 2:** *From what I remember. Like we all thought that we were know-it-alls and we thought we had [what we needed] in the book and just didn't value it for so many different reasons.*

**Literacy Coach 1:** *And the resistance of, Why are we doing this? I have other things I need to do during this time. And, you know...now it's like the expectations are there. People are accustomed to meeting regularly. They know their grade-level time, and they get down to business. You know, I mean they know they just have those 40 minutes.*

**Literacy Coach 2:** *Like now...the literacy coordinator will come in with an agenda. It's very focused, and the teachers know what they're going to do at the meeting, what they're going to get out of it. And I feel like they know that they're going to get something out it. They don't view it as a waste of time.*

**Literacy Coach 1:** *[There was improvement] on both ends. On the teachers' end [and] on the literacy coach's, you know, the literacy teacher. This is from my perspective; they got better doing what they were doing and knowing that we're coming in. There's an agenda. We're not going to let you [complain] for 20 minutes and eat 20 minutes up of valuable time that we need to get things done. And then just everyone understanding [that] there was a benefit to a grade-level meeting. They were there for a purpose.*

**Literacy Coach 2:** *I absolutely agree.*

**Literacy Coach 1:** *Because I remember in the beginning, it was like we'd get in and there'd be a lot of just, you know, general chat. And then the next thing you know, it's like, I've got to get this done, and this done, and I need you to do this, and Oh, we [have] to go now, you know, prep is over. You know, so everybody became more focused in knowing how to do it.*

The early stages of development of the team meetings were challenging for both teachers and literacy coaches. The coaches were not sure about their role, how to conduct meetings, or how to develop the practices and protocols for successful meetings. Over time their experiences changed. The coaches reflected on how the meetings became something that they knew how to facilitate and that the teachers valued. One of the coaches acknowledged, "Grade-level meetings are like pretty much the core of how things happen." These reflections illustrate the learning curve the coaches experienced:

> **Literacy Coach 1:** *The person who was responsible for leading grade-level meetings [had] never attended one in her life. And never had any training on it. So it's like, okay meet every week...it definitely changed across time. Now it's like when the literacy coordinator goes in, the teachers go in. It's like okay—they already have their agenda. They already know everything that needs to be accomplished. They know, like, actions that they need to take before the next meeting, you know. So...it's a process.*

> **Literacy Coach 2:** *Yeah. It is. I mean, but there's a learning curve to everything.*

## Talking About Data

The standards-based approach to change that was central to my work with the teachers and coaches at South Loop set the stage for teacher conversations. The grade-level meetings were the vehicles through which teachers could talk about assessment, examine data, and make instructional decisions. The nature and content of these conversations are examined in detail in

"As teachers start meeting regularly, typical conversations may be superficial and touch on all aspects of teaching. Initially, many teachers use the time to air their feelings about school life. Because they aren't used to "conversing," they may have to get these general concerns out of the way first. It often takes more than a year for meetings to focus on curriculum and improving student learning. Additionally, many teachers are embarrassed to admit that they need help. They believe that everyone else must be a successful practitioner who already knows how to teach a particular skill or discipline."

—Routman (2002, 32)

Chapter 6. As the team meetings developed, did discussions about student achievement data take place during the meetings? In separate conversations, teachers and literacy coaches shared their thoughts about the school and its use of data.

> **Teacher:** *Since [the new administration] came, there has been a big push in general to use the data differently at this school or any school where I ever worked…We didn't get it and now that we get it…*

A literacy coach also remembered about data use at the school prior to 2003:

> **Literacy Coach:** *Like we didn't use to really analyze data, so we didn't—from what I remember, like, we didn't really look to see, like, where each grade level was on the ISAT and on the ITBS. So we didn't know where our strengths were at the school and what our weaknesses were.*

Although these statements make it clear that the teachers did not recall times when they analyzed student achievement data prior to 2003, they claimed that data was now used differently, looking at the strengths and weaknesses of the students.

The conversations about data changed over time as illustrated in Figure 4.9 on the following page. This figure illustrates that there were few or no routines or structures that supported teacher conversations about summative or formative assessment data in 2003. During this school year, conversations about assessment occurred, but they were neither ongoing nor comprehensive. These conversations, which began in February 2003, were instructional in nature—intended to help the teachers become familiar with some basics about assessment. Literacy coaches facilitated workshops for teachers who chose to meet after school. These workshops aimed to provide a general awareness about the expectations of the upcoming Illinois State Achievement Test from the state. These workshops were grounded in the standards and the level of rigor expected of students on high-stakes tests, which were scheduled for March of that year, just a few short weeks away.

In 2004, routines for working with assessments and assessment data were put in place. In grade-level team meetings, held three times a year, teachers examined schoolwide assessment data. By the end of that school year, assessment data were used for schoolwide curriculum planning. In addition to these activities, teachers collaboratively scored writing assessments and gave data presentations at schoolwide gallery walks. All these activities were ongoing after 2004.

**Figure 4.9. The Role of Assessment and Assessment Data 2003–2006**

| August 2002–June 2003 | August 2003–June 2004 | August 2004–June 2005 | August 2005–June 2006 |
|---|---|---|---|
| • ISAT Assessment Preparation for Exploratory Writing (02/03)<br>• ISAT Assessment Preparation for Narrative Writing (02/03)<br>• ISAT Assessment Preparation for Reading Extended Response (03/03) | • Schoolwide Assessment, Scoring & Analysis in Grade-Level Teams (10/03, 01/04, 03/04)<br>• Gallery Walk: Schoolwide Assessment and Data Presentations (10/03, 01/04, 03/04)<br>• Teachers Begin Collaboratively Scoring Student Writing (01/04)<br>• Assessment Data Informs Schoolwide Curriculum Planning (06/04) | • Schoolwide Professional Development Supports Data Discussions Across Grade-Level Teams (09/04)<br>• Schoolwide Assessment, Scoring & Analysis in Grade-Level Teams (11/04, 01/05, 05/05)<br>• Gallery Walk: Schoolwide Assessment and Data Presentations (11/04, 01/05, 05/05) | • Schoolwide Assessment, Scoring & Analysis in Grade-Level Teams (09/05, 01/06, 05/06)<br>• Gallery Walk: Schoolwide Assessment and Data Presentations (09/05, 01/05, 05/06) |

## Consortium on Chicago School Research (CCSR) Survey

The CCSR began as a way to study the restructuring of the district in 1990. Researchers from the University of Chicago, the district, and other districts came together to study Chicago school reform. In 1991, CCSR began to survey schools (Sebring, Allensworth, Bryk, Easton, and Luppescu 2006). These results provide school-specific data about the degree to which key stakeholders perceive their involvement in five categories known as the essential supports:

- the school's instructional program
- professional learning community
- the school environment or climate
- leadership
- relationships with parents

Surveys are optional and can be conducted every two years, and data are made available to the principal at the school. The principal decides how school survey data are disseminated.

> "…looking at student achievement results in conjunction with the context of the school and the processes that create the results give teachers and administrators important information about what they need to do to improve learning for all students."
> —Victoria L. Bernhardt (2003, 30)

South Loop participated in the CCSR survey during the 2003, 2005, and 2007 school years. The school coordinator, lead teacher, or the school counselor administered the survey to ensure that it was free from influence from the school administration. The survey was optional, and teachers typically completed it in place of a staff meeting. These data illustrate a change in teacher perceptions over the course of this case study: data from the first and last years (2003 and 2007, respectively) were selected for analysis. Seventeen of 22 teachers completed the survey in the spring of 2003, and 26 of 28 teachers completed the survey in the spring of 2007. Teacher trust and program coherence were two areas surveyed. Results from these surveys are discussed in the following sections of this chapter.

## Change in Perceptions of Teacher Trust

A climate of trust and mutual respect is essential to the success of teacher meetings and collaborative efforts to improve teaching and learning. Data from the 2003 and 2007 CCSR surveys provided insight into the attitudes of South Loop teachers toward one another. The results reveal how teacher trust changed between 2003 and 2007. For those teachers completing the survey in 2003, 50% reported that they trusted colleagues. By 2007 the results shifted, with over 95% of the South Loop teachers surveyed reporting their trust in one another.

A professional learning community was evolving as teachers worked together to fulfill a vision for the school, a vision that contributed to dramatic changes in South Loop culture and student achievement.

## Change in Perceptions of Program Coherence

Providing new instructional materials was an initial step in creating curriculum consistency within and across the grades. We used a survey from the Consortium on Chicago School Research (CCSR) to learn about how well South Loop addressed program coherence.

The scale for this section of the survey assesses the degree to which teachers perceived that programs at their school are coordinated with each other and are consistent with common goals, both within and across grade levels. The results studied were from surveys administered in 2003 and again in 2007. The results, shown in Figure 4.10 on the following page, reveal that teachers' perceptions about curriculum consistency changed over this four-year period. South Loop results are shown in comparison to average results from the district. Graphic representations of these data are included in Appendix 4.5 (p. 165) and Appendix 4.6 (p. 166).

The specific responses to each of the seven items on this scale show that in 2003, South Loop teachers' ratings were below the district average. While all questions illustrate how teachers perceived South Loop, two questions in particular show the impact that the constant turnover in school administration had on these teachers and the school: 29% of the teachers reported that new programs, once started, are followed up on; 26% reported that coordination and focus on instruction had changed for the better over the last two years.

Responses to this section of the 2007 survey compared to the same section of the 2003 survey show considerable change in how teachers report their perceptions of their school. Specific responses to the same questions cited above from the 2003 survey show that in 2007, 88% of the teachers reported that new programs, once started, were followed up on; and 96% reported that coordination and focus on instruction had changed for the better over the last two years.

**Figure 4.10. South Loop Program Coherence Survey Results, 2003 and 2007.**

| Program Coherence Survey Items | SLES 2003 | District 2003 | SLES 2007 | District 2007 |
|---|---|---|---|---|
| **Teachers agree that in this school...** | | | | |
| You can see continuity from one program to another | 18% | 53% | 68% | 61% |
| Many special programs [do not] come and go | 31% | 53% | 72% | 59% |
| Once we start a new program, we follow up with it | 29% | 66% | 88% | 73% |
| Curriculum and instruction are well coordinated across the grades | 35% | 64% | 88% | 70% |
| We [do not] have so many programs that I can't keep track | 41% | 59% | 42% | 64% |
| Curriculum and instruction are consistent among teachers in the same grade | 58% | 76% | 76% | 81% |
| Coordination/focus of instruction has changed for the better in the last two years | 26% | 59% | 96% | 65% |

Number of SLES Teachers Responding: 2003: 17 out of 22; 2007: 26 out of 28.

Teacher perception about school coherence between 2003 and 2007 changed considerably over those four years. However, it is also important to compare the change at South Loop against changes at other schools in the district to understand the change at the school within the context of the district. Data from the CCSR survey provides a lens for such comparisons. Comparative data are shown in Figure 4.11 below. As previously shown (Figure 4.10), responses on the 2003 survey were below the district averages. These data illustrate how low the scale was for South Loop during 2003 compared to other schools in the district. The change over four years is dramatic: in 2007, South Loop ranks above the aggregated data for all schools in the district program coherence. These comparisons are shown in Figure 4.11. All CPS schools are represented by the solid line and black circles. The dashed line with asterisks represents schools similar to South Loop; the dashed line with stars represents South Loop.

**Figure 4.11. Program Coherence, 1999–2007: Individual School Survey Report**

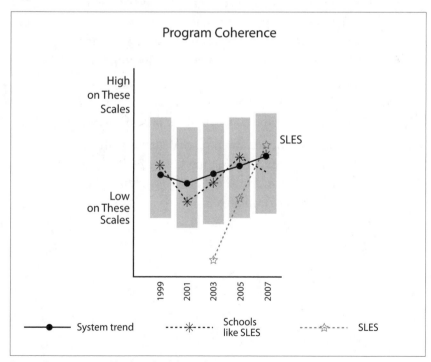

Source: Consortium on Chicago School Research, 2007.

## A Picture of Change Emerges

The actions described in this chapter provide a glimpse into the changes occurring at South Loop. Teachers could see the benefits of standards-based instruction and formative assessment through the changes in student achievement. They and the coaches were becoming more at ease in participating in grade-level meetings. The culture of the school was changing as teachers became more trusting of one another. Experiences recorded in the professional literature and shared anecdotally remind us of the positive effects of collegial conversations and a commitment to shared values and goals. My colleagues and I at South Loop were acquiring our own stories about the process of change. More of this story comes in the next chapter, where you can find out about the conversations we had about data, teaching, and learning.

## Reflection: Thinking About Teaching and Learning

1. From the chapter, select one quotation that best represents your perspective about actions that lead to change. Share your observations about the quotation with colleagues, or jot down some thoughts in your professional learning journal.

2. Look back at the remarks of the teachers (p. 86) and literacy coaches (pp. 87–90). What themes do you see expressed in these remarks? Describe comparable experiences you have had.

3. Describe your experiences with grade-level meetings or other settings in which teachers come together to talk about teaching and learning. What makes these events worthwhile? What makes them counter-productive?

# Chapter 5

## *Teacher Conversations Foster Change*

In the previous chapter, I included several transcripts of recollections from teachers and coaches recorded in focus group sessions conducted in 2007 as part of data collection for my case study of South Loop Elementary School. These candid observations about experiences prior to and including 2003 offer insights into some aspects of the school climate as it affected faculty: teacher isolation, anxiety about participating in a grade-level team meeting, recognition that a real vision for the school was being offered, and growing pains associated with the development of grade-level team meetings. These circumstances began to change as teachers became involved with formative assessment practices, saw evidence of improvements in student achievement, and engaged in collaborative work.

Creating the conditions for collaborative effort can be a challenge, but it was increasingly evident that teachers and coaches were willing to meet the challenge. Teachers were engaged in discussions about formative assessment data and talked about the use of rubrics to assess student writing. Gallery Walks provided opportunities for teachers to demonstrate instructional strategies and talk about them. Development of school improvement plans allowed teachers to formalize decisions based on standards and assessment data and demonstrated that structures and routines were in place at the school. Such activities afforded teachers many opportunities to talk about and reflect on their practices. Productive work was central to these activities that sustained commitment to accomplishing the primary goal of improving student achievement through effective

"When school faculties develop the skills of dialogue and discussion, they learn how to transform their talk into meaningful communication that improves relationships and makes a real difference for student learning."

— Garmston and Wellman (1998, 30)

practice. Talking with colleagues about teaching and learning was inescapable during these activities.

## Examining Student Achievement Data

In September 2003, the school began to use formative assessments in reading comprehension and writing. Grounded in the expectations of state standards, these assessments were developed to engage teachers in student work—reading, writing, and problem solving—and also to engage students in the level of rigor that was expected of them at their grade level. When asked if there was a time when the school started to get better at using data and data analysis, the literacy coaches responded affirmatively.

> **Literacy Coach 2:** *Oh, definitely year three [2005] …Like [Literacy Coach 1] was saying about breaking them up into—what—okay, this is a multiple choice question, what is this question asking? You know, is it like an inferential question or whatever. So that was the first time I think we really dissected.*
>
> **Literacy Coach 1:** *And…is there a pattern emerging? You know, are children better answering the explicit questions versus the implicit, and really understanding?*
>
> **Literacy Coach 2:** *And not just like talking, like, "Okay, this child scored an A."*
>
> **Literacy Coach 1:** *Eight out of 10.*
>
> **Literacy Coach 2:** *This child scored a C. You know, it's like, okay well, eight out of 10—what are they struggling with?*
>
> **Literacy Coach 1:** *Right. I mean, really analyzing it and understanding what you're doing.*
>
> **Literacy Coach 2:** *I'd say the starting point was year three [2005]…*

Teachers also engaged in discussions about using rubrics to assess student writing. This work was also considered to be an analysis of student achievement data. One teacher recalls a time during 2006 when the grade-level team collaboratively scored student work.

> **Teacher:** *You don't really know for 100 percent sure 'is this a three?' It is quality. We have to really talk among ourselves and that's what we don't have time to do. That's an issue at the grade level...you and your teachers in your same grade need time to sit down for a while and discuss: Look at this one—how is this looking to you? It takes hours to grade those things.*

The teacher states her frustration and the lack of time during grade-level team meetings for teachers to score student work. However, the teacher does not express frustration about doing the work or about collaborating with colleagues, or the conversation they were engaged in about the quality of student writing. The discussion continued, and the teachers talked about how the process of using formative assessment affected what happened during grade-level team meetings.

> **Teacher 1:** *I feel like it started a strategy now [2006].*
>
> **Teacher 2:** *It was a lot better this year...I think they heard us last year because last year we complained a great deal about the fact that grade-level meetings are not our own and they are not supposed to be. And this year, they still had their little to-do lists, but it seemed like they would be able to sit down and look over [student work]. It is never enough time, but they tried a little more this year to give us time to actually sit and look at data with your partner and not have four other things that you have to do in an hour. Do you know what I mean? It is better. It is not where it should be. But it is a lot better, and I think they tried more this year.*

> "The analysis of student work over time with written analyses and reflections is one of the most powerful ways to improve the 'perennial skill' of the effective teacher: the ability to analyze a student's progress in light of a well-defined learning target and determine which teaching approaches might best help the student grow."
> —Langer, Colton, and Goff (2003, 127)

The discussions among teachers and coaches about assessments and results were embedded in practice. Together they were reviewing student performance, comparing student work, and considering what they were doing instructionally.

## School Gallery Walks

School Gallery Walks were instituted in October 2003. Designed to provide another forum in which teachers engaged in data discussions, the Gallery Walks included grade-level team displays and presentations about student achievement related to specific learning benchmarks from state standards. I provided guidelines to assist teachers in preparing to present and discuss data in the Gallery Walk. Following is an example:

**Figure 5.1 Gallery Walk Guideline Sample**

Tuesday, September 27th is South Loop's first Gallery Walk of the year. We will start our restructured day in the Auditorium by reviewing displays of grade-level boards, assessment data, and curriculum guides. During this short session, teachers will have the opportunity to visit each grade-level table and learn about the great things going on in our school.

Next, each grade level will be responsible for presenting a five-minute report at our Gallery Walk. Comprehension and math extended response will be the focuses during the reporting sessions. The following questions should be addressed during each report:

- How did your students perform on the assessments?
- What surprised you about the results?
- What areas concern you?
- What patterns or trends do you notice?
- What do you need to carry out your plan?

While your colleagues are reporting on their grade-level assessments, classroom teachers will provide written feedback about student strengths, areas of concern, questions, and suggestions about instructional strategies. At the conclusion of the gallery walk, teacher teams will receive this written feedback to review during grade-level team meetings.

The school scheduled three Gallery Walks per school year, as shown below in Figure 5.2. One walk was at the start of the school year, the next one was at the end of the first semester, and the last one was before the end of the school year.

**Figure 5.2. South Loop Elementary School Gallery Walk and Formative Assessments, 2003–2006**

| Gallery Walk Date | Formative Assessments Discussed During the Gallery Walk | Formative Assessments Administered |
|---|---|---|
| 10-06-03 | Comprehension, Writing | Comprehension, Writing |
| 01-29-04 | Comprehension, Writing | Comprehension, Writing |
| 03-26-04 | Comprehension, Writing | Comprehension, Writing |
| 11-02-04 | Comprehension, Writing | Comprehension, Writing, Fluency, Math Problem Solving |
| 01-28-05 | Comprehension, Writing | Comprehension, Writing, Fluency, Math Problem Solving |
| 05-27-05 | Comprehension, Writing | Comprehension, Writing, Fluency, Math Problem Solving |
| 09-27-05 | Comprehension, Math Problem Solving | Comprehension, Writing, Fluency, Math Problem Solving |
| 01-27-06 | Comprehension, Math Problem Solving | Comprehension, Writing, Fluency, Math Problem Solving |
| 05-26-06 | Comprehension, Math Problem Solving | Comprehension, Writing, Fluency, Math Problem Solving |

The Gallery Walks were grounded in the Standards-Based Change Process and marked the beginning of schoolwide public discourse about data. The impact is evident in comments from one teacher:

> **Teacher:** *We shared strategies more, where before I might only hear what seventh grade is doing in a Gallery Walk or even other people in my cluster. And now in grade-level meetings we share actual strategies that we are using in our classrooms. So it is more time to communicate with people where I didn't have that before, so it is handing over more a little bit…Things need to be worked on to improve it but we were talking more and sharing strategies, not just how we were improving assessments but just overall classroom but different content and how that was working and that was helpful.*

Literacy coaches had a role in developing the Gallery Walks and observing changes that occurred as teachers became more in tune with analyzing data and instructional strategies. A literacy coach recalled:

> **Literacy Coach:** *…Gallery Walks in the beginning really were— they were just like boards and people walked around and like looked at them, and then they got much more public, and then I think that's probably when the shift started happening too, because it's fine to [think that] no one will read [it] anyway. [But to] stand and be like, This is what I did; This is why I did it; Does anyone have any questions? And someone was like, Well, why are [we] doing that in fifth grade when I'm doing it in second grade? That's much different for a teacher even if they didn't buy into the process.*

The Gallery Walks underwent two changes—one in format and the other in discussion. The format change from display boards to teacher presentation required peers to stand before one another and present their students' work and achievement data in bar graphs, as well as plans to target the learning needs of students in their grade levels. The teachers also described the key learning outcomes that the assessment addressed and how the assessment was evaluated. Figure 5.3 on the following pages shows the school documents outlining the steps that were essential before, during, and after each Gallery Walk.

**Figure 5.3. Gallery Walk Documents**

The In-School Gallery Walk is a critical event moving toward a coherent literacy program. It provides a site for the school staff as a whole to hear what their students are able to do in terms of end-of-year expectations. It helps staff hear the range of assessments in each grade level. It makes visible how each grade level is contributing to the school's vision of the excellent graduating reader. These are the reasons why it is one of the core expectations for each school for Year 3 in Partnership READ.

Teachers administer the assessments during the schoolwide assessment dates for fall, winter, and spring. For each cycle, individual teachers administer the agreed-upon assessments within their grade levels to their students. This happens within a common period of time as determined by the principal. The cycle includes time to administer the classroom assessments, for teachers to talk with one another at each grade level about their students' work (using the rubrics and other scoring tools) and implications for instruction, time to prepare their grade level's presentation to the school, and time for the whole school to share their presentations.

### Preparing for the Gallery Walk

These are the formal "steps" to the In-School Gallery Walk:

- Teachers are to administer their assessments in their classrooms. The assessments relate to each of the end-of-year "I Cans" in each of the areas targeted: comprehension, writing, fluency, math, and extended response.

- Teachers are to meet together in grade-level groups to talk about the results of the assessment. This includes scoring the students' work together—trading papers from each other's classrooms as well as evaluating how well the rubric is working. It includes time to talk about the results of the assessment in terms of implications for instruction: the potential strategies and materials to use to meet students' needs. It includes time to evaluate the quality of information from the assessment and whether it should be tweaked before using again.

- Each grade-level team is to prepare a presentation, deciding who will do what for each grade level's presentation to the staff and preparing a display board for an In-School Gallery Walk.

**Figure 5.3. Gallery Walk Documents** *(cont.)*

### The Presentation at the Gallery Walk

Each grade-level presentation should capture what the grade level is doing to contribute to the vision of the literate graduate. This includes the following:

- the "I cans" that are driving the assessment choices and how these "I cans" contribute to the overall school vision
- the assessment used for each "I can" and how it was evaluated (key areas)
- the results of the grade level
- the bar graphs that display the distribution
- what the bar graphs mean for decisions about how to meet students' needs
- the instructional plans (i.e., the strategies and the materials likely to be used) between now and the next Gallery Walk based on the results of the assessments

The School Gallery Walks provided settings in which teachers engaged in collaborative conversations. The structure helped focus talk on teaching and learning—it was embedded in the practice of the school. The guidelines for presentation helped teachers to think carefully about what was happening with their students. Time in the school day and time in the school year allowed teachers and coaches to work as teams—reviewing student work, comparing student work from different classes, and talking about strategies and why some seem to work more effectively than others.

## School Improvement Plan

School improvement plans have become essential documents in school reform efforts. The School Improvement Plan for Advancing Academic Achievement (SIPAAA) provides descriptive data about the structures and routines that were established for the use of assessments and data serving as the basis for teacher conversations about teaching and learning. All Chicago Public Schools are required to submit a SIPAAA to the district, demonstrating how findings from a school internal review lead to priority goals, strategies, activities, and the school's budget for the upcoming two school years. Given the evidence from data thus far, it is reasonable to expect to see supportive data with a focus on assessments, data analysis, and curriculum planning.

> "A growing body of evidence suggests that when teachers collaborate to pose and answer questions informed by data from their own students, their knowledge grows and their practice changes."
> — David (2009, 87)

The 2006–2008 SIPAAA, developed during 2006, provided evidence of the structures and routines that were established at South Loop. One of four priorities was to meet performance targets in reading, with a particular emphasis on closing the achievement gap between subgroups. Similar priorities were set for math and science, respectively. Two strategies, developed to move the school toward these priority goals, illustrated the focus the SIPAAA planning team intended for the work that was ahead:

- Teachers and students will increase the use of rubrics to assess the quality of student work and revise products to meet the benchmark.
- Teachers will continue to administer standards-based assessments in comprehension, writing, and fluency, and report the findings three times a year.

The activity section in the SIPAAA outlines the key actions determined by the SIPAAA planning team to support the strategy and the priority goal (see Figure 5.4 on the following page). Statements like "increase the use of rubrics" and "continue to administer assessments" as strategies demonstrate that the use of assessments and data that lead to conversations about curriculum planning was not new to the school. Similarly, the SIPAAA activities outlined the structures and routines that the school agreed to continue to implement.

**Figure 5.4. South Loop Elementary School 2006–2008 SIPAAA Selected Activities**

Activities:

A. Teachers will administer standards-based assessments in comprehension, writing, and fluency, and report the findings three times a year (through Gallery Walks).

B. Teachers will utilize formative assessments to develop and modify quarterly standards-based curriculum maps that reflect the student learning needs.

C. Teachers will work collaboratively in grade-level meetings to plan differentiated instruction and to seek reading resources designed to support student-learning needs.

D. Teachers will utilize proven, data-driven strategies that the grade-level team has determined to be in line with students' individual needs.

E. Teachers will work collaboratively and individually, utilizing standards-based assessment results to develop and modify instruction designed to move students to the end-of-the-year goals.

F. Project-based curriculum will be further developed to meet literacy standards.

G. Teachers will teach strategies that the grade-level team has determined to be effective for student achievement.

H. Teachers and students will use rubrics to assess the quality of student work and revise products to meet the benchmarks.

I. Teachers will document student work in standards-based portfolios, which will include formative assessments and integrated curricular projects.

J. Teachers will increase parent involvement in literacy instruction and the strategies and outcomes taught during each month through monthly newsletters.

K. Teachers will provide extended day support for students who are not proficient at grade level in reading.

L. Time for teacher professional development will be allocated during restructured or professional development days, grade-level meetings, and after school to further develop reading instruction strategies and curricular units that integrate core content across subject matter, fitness, and the arts.

M. Teachers will engage in professional development in the use of leveled books and a balanced literacy approach aimed at differentiated student instruction.

## Nature of Teacher Conversations

The routines involved in the school Gallery Walks and the requirements to be fulfilled for the School Improvement Plan complement one another. Each activity centers on formative assessment data, standards-based instruction, and collaborative discussions with colleagues. Gallery Walks, grade-level team meetings, and professional development sessions were regularly scheduled routines and rituals for the school during the fall, winter, and spring. Data from professional development sessions and grade-level team meetings show that these were also central to the school's work. Data from grade-level team meetings show that teachers engaged in several assessment and data discussions prior to each Gallery Walk. The need for grade-level teams to prepare for their part of the presentation at the schoolwide public event drove these discussions. For example, grade-level team minutes during 2005, the second year for the school's use of formative assessments, show discussions about administering assessments beginning September 9, 2004. The minutes from October, 2004 show that these assessments would be the focus of the upcoming Gallery Walk, on November 2, 2004. Teachers administered the assessments in order to acquire data for their public presentations, which also included making an instructional plan to move their students to expected outcomes. By October 7th, the grade-level team meeting agenda was titled "Presentation 11/2/04." The discussion topic for that day was titled "Nov. 2 (Institute Day) Teacher Presentations" (What you're doing in your classroom; strategies you're using in conjunction with what you've learned from Pre-assessments. Must touch on each component 5 to 10 min).

Data from grade-level team meeting minutes show teachers working out the process in preparation for the Gallery Walk. That year, the first assessment cycle began on September 9 and culminated with a Gallery Walk on November 2, almost a two-month process. The mention of an Institute Day in the minutes (schoolwide professional development days are often called Institute Days in CPS) shows the connection between schoolwide professional development days, meetings for grade-level teams, and the use of assessments. The sample grade-level team minutes in Appendix 5.1 (pp. 167–170) further illustrate the integrated nature of topics and activities.

A review of the annual professional development plans, the SIPAAA, and the flow of topics and activities for grade-level team meetings for 2004 through 2006 shows that there was coordination across these different days and meetings. The pattern or cycle that emerges from these data shows that teachers achieved the following:

- administered assessments three to eight weeks prior to a Gallery Walk (the time difference between the assessment and the Gallery Walk reduced significantly during 2005 and 2006)

- collaboratively discussed and scored the formative assessments (student work) in grade-level team meetings, during scheduled after-school planning time, and other times as needed

- developed and organized data based on the assessment results

- analyzed assessment data from the current assessments, as well as from assessment data over time

- used the analysis of the data to develop instructional plans during grade-level team meetings and during scheduled after-school planning time

- developed 10-minute presentations for the upcoming Gallery Walk (schoolwide public discussion), during grade-level team meetings, during scheduled after-school planning time, and other times as needed

- utilized input from colleagues following Gallery Walks to include key teaching strategies in instructional plans during grade-level team meetings and during scheduled after-school planning time

The work that occurred during schoolwide professional development days, as well as during grade-level team meetings, was coordinated, which provided structures and routines that came to be the foundation for assessment and data-related conversations. Sample data from grade-level team meeting minutes and school professional development plans illustrated how this was coordinated at the school. The professional development plan for 2005 provides an overview of the areas of focus and the sequence of events over the course of the school year (Appendix 5.2, pp. 171–172). Data from grade-level team minutes showed the same areas of focus and sequence of events for work done by grade-level teams, illustrating how the work teachers were engaged in during grade-level team meetings connected to the overall professional development plan for the school (Appendix 5.1, pp. 167–170). In addition, a visual representing this same cycle of assessment, data analysis, and instruction provided further evidence of how the flow of events described above were understood by the school administration and conveyed to the school community (Figure 5.5).

**Figure 5.5. South Loop Elementary School: Utilizing Ongoing Formative Assessments**

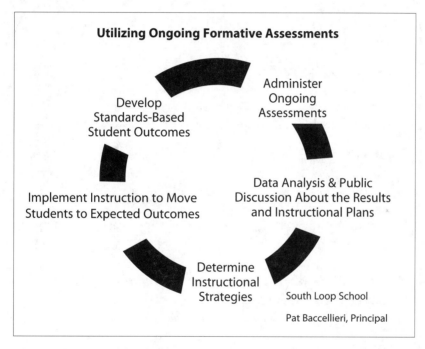

## *Impact of Collaborative Conversations*

The rituals and routines of assessment, data analysis, and instructional planning were central to the work of the school. Did these activities make a difference? I did not set out to prove that causality. However, it is useful to show both theory and evidence that would support such a causal interpretation. For example, if my hypothesis is that implementing data analysis and instructional planning are likely to improve student learning outcomes, and the implementation of such measures does indeed correlate with such outcomes, there is at least the plausibility in asserting causality. If teachers themselves believe that these measures made a difference in their teaching and that improvement in student learning resulted, then that plausibility is strengthened. In separate focus groups when the literacy coaches and teachers were discussing times where there may have been changes in what motivated them, their responses were similar. When asked if the improved ISAT scores had an impact, the literacy coaches responded with the following:

> **Literacy Coach 2:** *Absolutely. And there was also more pressure, more pressure to improve.*

> **Literacy Coach 1:** *Exactly. And also [to] keep the momentum going.*

> **Literacy Coach 2:** *What we're doing is working, kind of like that.*

> **Literacy Coach 1:** *Right, it's like that. It's rewarding to feel that all of this work has led to something, and there [are] concrete examples now…[that] the scores are increasing and the students are learning.*

When discussing what motivated her, one teacher remembered events at the start of 2007:

> **Teacher:** *This year the administration came in showing us the comparison between our school [ISAT data], the district, and the state so you could kind…of like…see where we are on the continuum.*

> *Even at one point they showed us that list of schools and where [our school was scoring in relation to other Chicago schools] and some thought we might be lower or higher, but I do like seeing some evidence…*

> *But what I like is seeing this vision. [The administration] can have a vision, but it somehow is a real thing, like the evidence that it is working and seeing the state, the district. We have always done at least the district scale or higher, and I kind of like that, seeing the evidence.*

During the same discussion, when asked if there were points at which some of the improvements in outcomes started to show up and, if yes, if that changed the climate or morale a little bit, another teacher responded with the following:

**Teacher:** *Yes. Once I saw a gain [in test scores], I believed in the vision, but once I saw it as a tangible thing, you know what I mean? That does kind of help you because you want to maintain that as your motivation. I will mention that I made a note here that last year's [2006] gains were kind of crazy. They were phenomenal, and when I saw these—followed them in the newspaper [during the summer]—I thought, uh-oh, because I anticipated our workload, which is already a lot,...was going to like triple, which it didn't, by the way.*

*I [anticipated that the administration would come] in and [say] we did this, [and] here are 10 more things to do. They kind of said, We: did this—let's make sure we maintain this level of excellence. And that I could appreciate because there was no more work I could have done. And I can change it and do something different that's better, but you couldn't have given me 10 more things to do...*

These comments provide evidence to support the assertion that "teacher conversations foster change." Here we see teachers following through on a commitment to improve student achievement by changing their approaches to the use of data and building a collaborative school culture. The task of school change became a group effort that took advantage of structures and routines in which we could all engage in deep conversations about teaching and learning.

"...if groups have a disposition to embrace community in pursuit of instructional improvement and to embrace investigation of their own assumptions and practices toward that end, then community can be transformational."
—Little in an interview with Crow (2008, 54)

## Reflection: Thinking About Teaching and Learning

1. From the chapter, select one quotation that best represents your perspective about the role and impact of teacher conversations. Share your observations about the quotation with colleagues, or jot down some thoughts in your professional learning journal.

2. Look back at the remarks of the literacy coaches (pp. 98, 102, 110) and teachers (pp. 99, 102, 110–111). In what ways are the observations of these educators comparable to those of you and your colleagues?

3. Which activities in your school have been most effective in helping faculty come together to address issues in teaching and learning? How do your activities compare to those at South Loop Elementary School?

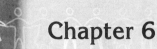

# Chapter 6

# A Professional Learning Community Evolves

Through this story of South Loop Elementary School's success, I am aiming to provide evidence that illustrates the critical role a professional learning community plays in supporting teachers and improving student achievement. Professional learning communities can have an enormous impact on teaching and learning: they are vehicles for strengthening instruction, which leads to improved student learning; they support teachers in acquiring new knowledge and skills; and they give teachers a voice in decision-making about assessment practices, curriculum materials, and how the school functions. The structures of the professional learning community were instrumental in providing a context in which South Loop leadership, teachers, and coaches became a *professional learning community* rather than a gathering of teachers in the faculty lounge, at a grade-level team meeting, or at a schoolwide professional development event. The structures included regularly scheduled grade-level team meetings, school Gallery Walks, a modified school schedule, focus on standards-based assessment, and curriculum consistency within and across the grades. In addition to scheduling key events, another structure was the expectation that teachers bring common student work samples or assessment data to these scheduled meetings and events. While such structures are important, they are never sufficient to transform a school into a professional learning community. The culture of the school has to change—a challenge that is much more difficult than the decision to purchase a new reading and math series or to redesign the school schedule to give teachers time to meeting during the school day. School culture is characterized by trust, program coherence, acceptance of collective responsibility for change, and discussion supported by reflection. Eaker and Keating (2008) describe cultural shifts necessary to the development of a successful professional learning community: shift in fundamental purpose from teaching to learning; shift from teachers working in isolation to working in collaborative teams; and shift in focus to outcomes and results rather than inputs and intentions. In

> "Structural change that is not supported by cultural change will eventually be overwhelmed by the culture, for it is in the culture that the organization finds meaning and stability."
> —Schlechty (1997, 136)

previous chapters, I have described the cultural changes occurring as South Loop embarked on a standards-based approach to change: trust and respect for colleagues, acceptance of a new vision for the school, participation in collegial activities, acceptance of responsibility for using data to inform instruction, and pride in improvements in student achievement. These features were indicative of the professional learning community that evolved in the school over a five-year period. During this time I witnessed the integration of structural and cultural changes that demonstrated collective commitment to change. South Loop was experiencing a transformation.

## Coherence in the Work

Professional development plans, the school improvement plan, minutes from grade-level team meetings, and teacher comments illustrate high degrees of consistency and focus on student work and assessment data and instructional planning (see Chapter 5). The synergy among schoolwide professional development, grade-level team meetings, and teacher planning during after-school sessions illustrates a powerful and propelling continuous cycle. The school's professional development plan shows a consistent focus over the course of the year on assessment, data analysis, and curriculum planning. These topics were considered in cycles, beginning in the fall with assessment, then data analysis, then curriculum planning. This cycle was repeated in the winter and again in the spring. Agendas from grade-level team meetings showed that these meetings followed the same cycle: assessment, analysis, curriculum planning. The intersection of these topics embedded in various activities throughout the school year brought coherence to the work of the teachers and coaches. This process is illustrated below in Figure 6.1.

**Figure 6.1: Coherent Professional Focus**

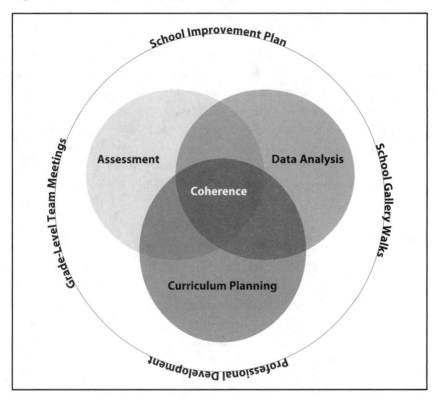

## Focus on Curriculum Planning

Teacher conversation is a central feature of events taking place within a professional learning community. In this context, conversation has an explicit purpose—to accomplish a specific objective, which at South Loop was making data-based decisions about instruction. "How did assessment data affect curriculum planning?" Answering this key question was at the center of my case study. School documents that are central to illustrating the nature of teacher conversations include minutes from grade-level team meetings (see Appendix 5.1, pp.

167–170); school professional development plans (see Appendix 5.2, pp. 171–172); survey results from the Consortium on Chicago School Research; and comments from teacher and literacy coach focus groups. The impact of conversations about student assessment data on curriculum planning is illustrated in these comments expressed in a literacy coach focus group:

> **Literacy Coach:** *You know, there [were] a lot of things going on. Like you give an assessment, you scored them, you talked about them, you analyzed them, and then it's time for the next…I think it affected instruction in the sense that, because we were understanding the assessments and what they contained, that teachers were tailoring instructions to meet the students weaknesses and their strengths. So if they're not getting, you know, say they're not understanding inferential questions, we're going to teach them inferencing…*

### Planning Collaboratively for Instruction

Preparing lesson plans and teaching are functions that teachers do individually and in teams. This work is, without a doubt, a core function for teachers. At South Loop, it took time for this work to become collaborative and for the engagement to take place in a meaningful way. One teacher recalled how things were prior to 2003:

> **Teacher:** *There was nothing consistent about anything in the school. Teachers did different things, and we didn't have grade-level things. You talked to your friend, teacher next door, [or] coworker informally, and we didn't really plan together. If somebody wanted to teach dinosaurs or the rainforest, they did it.*

Another teacher new to the school, just one year after grade-level meetings started, was surprised about what was in place at the school during her first year. During the course of a teacher focus group conversation, this teacher was surprised to find out that grade-level team meetings had started only one semester or six months prior to when she started at the school.

**Teacher 1:** *That says to me…it seemed like things were already there but it hadn't even been an entire year, that change can happen quickly without—you can have this huge end goal like [the administration] had, right, but you can start that process and have some good effective changes in place, already saved the lives in the school without reaching that end goal. You're immediately—the second you make the teachers have grade-level meetings, you are seeing effective changes. You know what I mean? It is not the kind of thing that's years away….The second [the administration] instituted one grade-level meeting, change began. That's what it says to me.*

**Teacher 2:** *But there weren't grade-levels our first year [2003].*

**Teacher 3:** *There were.*

**Teacher 4:** *There were.*

**Teacher 5:** *There were because I remember [the literacy coach] had to come to my classroom to get me for each one. I was scared and hiding at my desk.*

While grade-level teams met during 2003, the school schedule shows that the meetings began at the beginning of the second semester. Meetings were scheduled between January and June of 2003, yet teachers were unaccustomed to meeting and planning together, and as one teacher noted, she "was scared and hiding." However, the impact of the meetings was clear to the teacher who began teaching at the school for the 2003–2004 school year. When she realized that the grade-level meetings had been in place for only six months, she recognized how quickly things at the school had changed over one semester.

Collaborative planning is characterized by several features, including reflective dialogue, collective responsibility, and innovation. As part of my case study, I was interested in finding out about South Loop teachers' perceptions related to selected aspects

"…when teachers work by themselves to make sense of student assessment results, what they learn is unlikely to contribute to the creation of a coherent instructional program."
—Sharkey and Murnane (2003, 80)

of collaborative planning. To obtain this information, I examined data from three sections of these CCSR surveys on "Faculty Responses about Teaching and Student Learning": reflective dialogue, collective responsibility, and innovation. Completed during the spring of 2003 and the spring of 2007, these surveys provided windows into how teachers responded to questions about teaching and learning. Data from these surveys are discussed in the next three sections.

## Reflective Dialogue

Taking time to examine the nature of a problem is an aspect of discussion that fosters reflection and moves conversations beyond a quick fix. As teachers at South Loop delved more deeply into student assessment data and what the results indicated for instruction, they engaged in reflective dialogue. Richardson (2002) observes that reflection is the process through which educators can tap into their knowledge to improve practice. Participating in grade-level team meetings and school Gallery Walks provided opportunities for SLES teachers and coaches to share observations, experiences, and knowledge. *Did they talk about teaching and student learning in those situations?* For answers to this question, I looked at data on Reflective Dialogue from the CCSR survey "Faculty Responses about Teaching and Student Learning." The seven items about reflective dialogue reveal how much teachers talked about instruction and student learning. Looking back four years to 2003, 19 out of 22 teachers completed the survey. The following averages of the 2003 CCSR survey on Reflective Dialogue illustrate teacher agreement on the extent to which teachers "talk informally about instruction, share and discuss student work with other teachers, and discuss assumptions about student learning":

- 15% of the teachers disagreed or strongly disagreed, reporting "Almost None."
- 32% agreed, reporting "Occasionally" (less than two to three times a month).
- 42% agreed, reporting "Regular" (one to three times a month).
- 11% strongly agreed, reporting "Frequent" (almost daily).

In 2003, South Loop responses to six of the seven items on this scale show that six were rated below district average (see Figure 6.2 on the following page). The item "conversations about curriculum planning more than twice a month" directly responds to the topic, reflective dialogue, which was central to my case study. This item received the lowest response—44% of the teachers perceived that they engaged in "conversations about curriculum planning more than twice a month." When this survey was administered, South Loop teachers were still new to situations in which they came together to talk about curriculum planning.

In 2007, 26 out of 28 teachers completed this section on Reflective Dialogue. The following averages of the 2007 survey illustrate teacher agreement on the extent to which teachers "talk informally about instruction, share and discuss student work with other teachers, and discuss assumptions about student learning" (CCSR Survey, 2007).

- 3% of the teachers disagreed or strongly disagreed, reporting "Almost None"
- 18% agreed, reporting "Occasionally" (less than two to three times a month)
- 52% agreed, reporting "Regular" (one to three times a month)
- 27% strongly agreed, reporting "Frequent" (almost daily)

The 2007 responses of South Loop teachers to seven of the seven items on this scale indicate that all responses were rated above the district average (Figure 6.2), showing ratings between 92 and 100 percent. These data are in sharp contrast to the data from the 2003 survey. Of particular interest here is the change in teachers' perceptions related to "conversations about curriculum planning more than twice a month." Ninety-two percent of the teachers perceived that they engaged in such conversations (Figure 6.2), an impressive change from results four years earlier. (Graphic representations of these data are shown in Appendix 6.1, p. 173, and Appendix 6.2, p. 174).

**Figure 6.2. South Loop and District Reflective Dialogue Survey Results, 2003 and 2007. Percent of Teachers Endorsing Each Statement.**

| Reflective Dialogue Survey Items | SLES 2003 | District 2003 | SLES 2007 | District 2007 |
|---|---|---|---|---|
| **Teachers report:** | | | | |
| Conversations about school's goals more than twice a month | 70% | 64% | 96% | 73% |
| Conversations about curriculum development more than twice a month | 44% | 64% | 92% | 73% |
| Conversations about managing class behavior more than twice a month | 82% | 83% | 92% | 87% |
| Conversations about what helps students learn best more than twice a month | 72% | 86% | 100% | 91% |
| Teachers regularly discuss assumptions about teaching and learning | 57% | 77% | 96% | 86% |
| Teachers share and discuss student work with other teachers | 68% | 81% | 96% | 88% |
| Teachers talk about instruction in the teachers' lounge | 68% | 80% | 100% | 88% |

Source: Consortium on Chicago School Research. 2003 and 2007.

Engaging teachers in conversations about student work on assessments, assessment data, and curriculum was central to the structures and routines that SLES was implementing. Through the survey results, teachers' perception that they talked about instruction changed from 44% in 2003 to 92% in 2007. These data support comments teachers made during the focus group, as well as information in minutes from grade-level team meetings. These discussions—the formal ones in grade-level team meetings and the informal ones—were core to the continuous cycles of improvement implemented at South Loop.

## Collective Responsibility

Acceptance of collective responsibility for improving teaching and learning is an important characteristic of a professional learning community. The CCSR survey section on Collective Responsibility determines the extent of shared commitment among faculty to improve the school so that all students learn. Data from surveys completed in the spring of 2003 and spring of 2007 provide insights into changes in South Loop teachers' perceptions about collective responsibility.

In 2003, 17 out of 22 teachers responded to this part of the survey. The following averages of the 2003 survey on Collective Responsibility illustrate "the extent of shared commitment among the faculty to improve the school so that all students learn" (CCSR Survey, 2003):

- 32% of the teachers claim that none or about half of their colleagues feel responsible that all students learn.

> "Dialogue is a reflective learning process in which group members seek to understand one another's viewpoints and deeply held assumptions. The word *dialogue* comes from the Greek *dialogos*. *Dia* means "through" and *logos* means "the word." In this process of "meaning making through words," group members inquire into their own and one another's beliefs, values, and mental models to better understand how things work in their world."
>
> —Garmston and Wellman (1998, 30)

- 26% of the teachers claim that about half of their colleagues feel responsible that all students learn.

- 23% of the teachers claim that most of their colleagues feel responsible that all students learn.

- 18% of the teachers claim that most or nearly all of their colleagues feel responsible that all students learn.

That year, South Loop responses to each of the seven items on this scale show that all were rated below district average. One item in this section had particular relevance. Responses to that item would provide insights into how teachers perceived collective responsibility. That item received the lowest response where 17% of the teachers perceived that they "take responsibility for improving the school" (see Figure 6.3 on the following page).

In 2007, 26 out of 28 teachers completed the section of the survey. The following averages of the 2007 survey on Collective Responsibility illustrate "the extent of shared commitment among the faculty to improve the school so that all students learn" (CCSR Survey, 2007):

- 5% of the teachers claim that none or about half of their colleagues feel responsible that all students learn.

- 19% of the teachers claim that about half of their colleagues feel responsible that all students learn.

- 47% of the teachers claim that most of their colleagues feel responsible that all students learn.

- 29% of the teachers claim that most or nearly all of their colleagues feel responsible that all students learn.

South Loop responses to seven of the seven items on this scale show that all responses were rated above the district average (Figure 6.3). In contrast to the 2003 responses to the item relevant to my case study, these data illustrate that 84% of the teachers perceived that they "take responsibility for improving the school" (Figure 6.3).

The 2003 and 2007 results for SLES and the district are shown in Figure 6.3. (Graphic representations of these results are provided in Appendix 6.3, p. 175, and Appendix 6.4, p. 176).

**Figure 6.3. SLES and District Collective Responsibility Survey Results, 2003 and 2007. Percent of Teachers Endorsing Each Statement.**

| Collective Responsibility Survey Items | SLES 2003 | District 2003 | SLES 2007 | District 2007 |
|---|---|---|---|---|
| **Most teachers in this school:** | | | | |
| Feel responsible when students fail | 41% | 49% | 60% | 57% |
| Feel responsibility to help each other do their best | 50% | 54% | 72% | 64% |
| Help maintain discipline in the entire school | 41% | 51% | 57% | 58% |
| Take responsibility for improving the school | 17% | 53% | 84% | 64% |
| Feel responsible for helping students develop self-control | 35% | 61% | 84% | 70% |
| Set high standards for themselves | 41% | 66% | 96% | 75% |
| Feel responsible that all students can learn | 47% | 68% | 92% | 77% |

Source: Consortium on Chicago School Research. 2003 and 2007.

Central to the structures and routines that were developed and fostered at South Loop was the notion that engaging teachers in shared examination of multiple sources of data on their students' learning progress provides an environment for teacher learning about the learning needs of students, thus making collaborative planning about improved curriculum, instruction, and assessment more likely. The idea that teachers report different responses about the responsibility assumed for improving the school between 2003 and 2007 indicates that teacher collaboration increased over these four years. Through the survey results, teachers affirm that they changed in the degree of responsibility that they took for the school, from 17% in 2003 to 84% in 2007. This dramatic change illustrates that most of the teachers at South Loop in 2007 were engaged in a shared commitment to improve the school so that all students learn.

## Trends in Professional Capacity

The CCSR survey "Faculty Responses about Teaching and Student Learning" is available to all Chicago Public Schools. CCSR also provides data that schools can use comparatively across schools in the district. These data provide school leaders and their teams with a context to interpret their school's survey results. In both the categories of reflective dialogue and collective responsibility, South Loop was below the district average during 2003 (Figure 6.2 and Appendix 6.1). By 2007, South Loop was at the top of the scale for reflective dialogue, and equal to schools like South Loop for Collective Responsibility (Figure 6.3 on the previous page and Appendix 6.2 on p. 174). This comparative data are shown in Figure 6.4. on the following page. All CPS schools are represented by the solid lines and black circles; the dashed line with asterisks represents schools similar to South Loop; the dashed line with stars represents South Loop. These data illustrate district trends and trends for schools similar to South Loop, providing a context for the changes expressed on the CCSR survey by the teachers at South Loop.

"Professional learning communities acknowledge there is no hope in helping all students learn unless those within the school work collaboratively in a collective effort to achieve that fundamental purpose."
—Eaker and Keating (2008, 15)

**Figure 6.4. Reflective Dialogue and Collective Responsibility, 1999–2007: Individual School Survey Report**

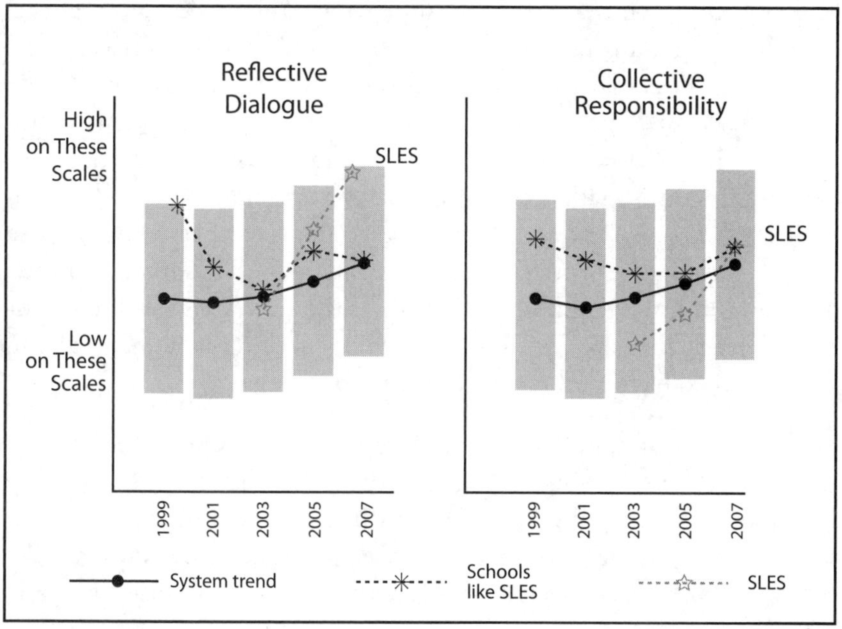

Source: Consortium on Chicago School Research 2007

I remember when the survey results from 2003 were mailed to my office. It affirmed that the challenges were real and that as a school we had a long way to go. I kept the team focused on implementing the systems, structures, and routines, with the belief that by repeatedly engaging teachers in the work, teachers would find value in collaborating. I knew that it was critical for South Loop to stay focused on the work and continue to expect 100 percent teacher participation in discussing assessments, reviewing assessment data, and planning curriculum. The 2007 results showed me that we were on the right track. I am not suggesting that any one strategy made the difference in the change in how teachers perceived their involvement at South Loop, but it is clear that there was a change, and that teachers and students benefited. The notion of collective responsibility for a common shared commitment to improve the school so all students learn is at the core of a professional learning community.

## Innovation

Innovation with a view to improving student achievement is central to capitalizing on teachers' growing knowledge and skill in a professional learning community. Several innovations were introduced at South Loop beginning in 2003 and continuing through 2007—formative assessments, standards-based curriculum, new reading and math series, grade-level team meetings, and school Gallery Walks. All of these changes called upon teachers to participate in new ways in the work of the school. The CCSR survey included a section on innovation. This section of the survey gauges the extent to which teachers are continually learning, seeking new ideas, acting as problem solvers, and are encouraged to change.

Seventeen out of 22 teachers responded to this section of the survey in 2003. The following averages of the 2003 survey on Innovation illustrate "whether teachers are continually learning and seeking ideas, have a 'can do' attitude, and are encouraged to change" (CCSR Survey, 2003). Averages have been rounded to the nearest whole number.

- 22% of the teachers report that none or some of the teachers in their school really try to improve their teaching, try new ideas, and take risks.

- 19% of the teachers report that about half of the teachers in their school really try to improve their teaching, and some try new ideas and take risks.

- 33% of the teachers report that about half or most of the teachers in their school really try to improve their teaching, and about half try new ideas and take risks.

- 27% of the teachers report that most or nearly all of the teachers in their school really try to improve their teaching, try new ideas, and take risks.

That year, South Loop responses to each of the six items on this scale show that all were rated below district average (Figure 6.5 on p. 128). One question in this section directly responds to the topic,

Innovation, illustrating that 35% of the teachers perceived that they were "eager to try new ideas."

In 2007, 26 out of 28 teachers completed the same section of the survey. Here are the results:

- 0% of the teachers report that none or some of the teachers in their school really try to improve their teaching, try new ideas, and take risks.

- 4% of the teachers report that about half of the teachers in their school really try to improve their teaching, and some try new ideas, and take risks.

- 26% of the teachers report that about half or most of the teachers in their school really try to improve their teaching, and about half try new ideas and take risks.

- More than 60% of the teachers report that most or nearly all of the teachers in their school really try to improve their teaching, try new ideas, and take risks.

The specific responses show that all South Loop responses were rated above the district average. 80% of the teachers perceived that they were eager to try new ideas.

The 2003 and 2007 results for South Loop and the district are shown in Figure 6.5. (Graphic representations of these data are shown in Appendix 6.5, p. 177, and Appendix 6.6, p. 178).

**Figure 6.5. South Loop and District Innovation Survey Results, 2003 and 2007. Percent of Teachers Endorsing Each Statement.**

| Innovation Survey Items | South Loop 2003 | District 2003 | South Loop 2007 | District 2007 |
|---|---|---|---|---|
| **Teachers agree that in this school:** | | | | |
| Most teachers are willing to take risks to make the school better. | 29% | 47% | 72% | 59% |
| Most teachers are eager to try new ideas. | 35% | 49% | 80% | 61% |
| Teachers have a "can do" attitude. | 70% | 82% | 92% | 88% |
| All teachers are encouraged to "stretch and grow." | 58% | 85% | 96% | 90% |
| Teachers are continually learning and seeking new ideas. | 70% | 85% | 100% | 91% |
| Most teachers are really trying to improve their learning. | 47% | 65% | 92% | 75% |

Source: Consortium on Chicago School Research. 2003 and 2007.

Similar to the concept of collective responsibility, innovation is also at the core of work that was embedded within the structures and routines that developed at South Loop. Again, the notion of engaging teachers in shared examination of multiple sources of data on their students' learning progress provides an environment for teacher learning about the learning needs of students, thus making collaborative planning about improved curriculum, instruction, and assessment more likely. Teacher innovation is critical to this work, as innovation is an essential component to collaborative teacher curriculum planning. The idea that assessment data drives instruction was one idea introduced to the teachers through the Standards-Based Change Process. As a result of the practices implemented at the school, teachers were empowered to work in teams and to solve problems—the problem at the core of this work was the problem of student underachievement. By working together in grade-level team meetings, teachers collaboratively developed plans to address their students' needs. The fact that teachers report different responses about how they were continually learning and seeking ideas between 2003 and 2007 indicates that teacher perception on their engagement in innovation increased over these four years. Survey data report (for 2003 and 2007 respectively) that 35%, then 80% of the teachers perceived that they were eager to try new ideas (Figure 6.5 on the previous page).

The survey results for innovation show trends similar to the comparative data obtained for reflective dialogue and collective responsibility. South Loop was considerably below CPS schools during 2003 and made significant gains by 2007. The 2007 survey data demonstrates that 92% of the teachers perceived that "most teachers are really trying to improve their teaching" and that 100% of the "teachers are continually learning and seeking new ideas." These perceptions and responses report comparatively high responses to the notion and activities involved in continuous learning, trust, and commitment.

As with collective responsibility and reflective dialogue, this dramatic change in teacher practice around the concept of innovation illustrates that most of the teachers at South Loop in 2007 perceived that they were engaged in a shared commitment to improve the school so that all students learn. Figure 6.6 on the following page shows this change. All CPS schools are represented by the solid line with circles; the dashed line with asterisks represents schools similar to South Loop; and the dashed line with stars represents South Loop.

> "Without change there is no innovation, creativity, or incentive for improvement. Those who initiate change will have a better opportunity to manage the change that is inevitable."
> —Pollard (n.d.)

**Figure 6.6. Innovation: 1999–2007. 2007 Individual School Survey Report**

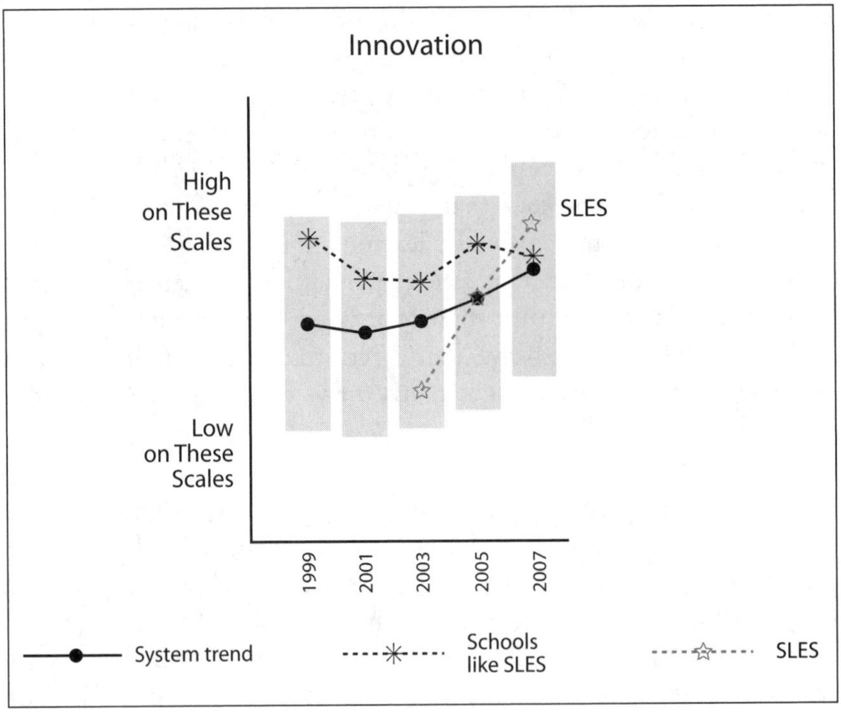

Source: Consortium on Chicago School Research, 1999–2007

## Curriculum Planning Accelerates

Over time the conversation began to change; however, the focus and depth of these conversations during the early years of the reform were not explicitly on curriculum. A review of agendas of the school professional development plans as it relates to this study illustrates the focus for professional development at the school (see Appendix 5.2 for topics in the 2005 school year, pp. 171–172). A review of the professional development shows that some workshops were focused on assessments, assessment data, and curriculum, while others were solely on assessments, some were on assessment data, and others were on curriculum. Between September 2002 and June 2004, 16 professional development workshops were focused on assessments, assessment data, and/or curriculum planning. Four of the 16 workshops included curriculum or curriculum planning as the focus, and two of those four days were in June 2004. Between July 2004 and July 2006, 25 workshops were focused on assessments, assessment data, and/or curriculum planning. Nineteen of the 25 workshops specifically engaged teachers in curriculum planning (see Figure 6.7 below).

**Figure 6.7. Professional Development Workshops that Addressed Assessments, Data, and/or Curriculum Planning**

| Year | Total Workshops | Assessments | Assessment Data | Curriculum Planning |
|------|-----------------|-------------|-----------------|---------------------|
| SY03–SY04 | 16^ | 15 | 6 | 4 |
| SY05–SY06 | 25^ | 11 | 19 | 19 |

^Some workshops addressed multiple topics.

Following the pattern set by the school agenda, the evolution of the school's focus shifted towards curriculum and instruction. One teacher reminded her colleagues about the concentration on curriculum:

**Teacher:** *During …the summer of 2004…that's [when] a lot of behind-the-scenes work [small teams who engaged in program and curriculum planning]…is going on…your whole thing isn't going to be successful without that behind-the-scenes work.*

The literacy coaches discussed curriculum mapping:

**Literacy Coach 1:** *[Curriculum mapping]…was handled all in two years [2005 and 2006]. We did like the bare bones of curriculum mapping after the first year [2003]…like the [reading standards] curriculum map. But yeah, the last two years [2005 and 2006].*

**Literacy Coach 2:** *…we started with the science and social studies mapping and then we worked on that over the summer [of 04]. [Now, it is] pretty much…all set in place.*

## Teacher Reflections of Change in Conversations and Practices

From time to time over the years, there was a need for reteaching. Even though the school was clear about the importance of the implementation of a standards-based curriculum, when the administration set the task of mapping social sciences and science, teachers often reverted to past practices. One literacy coach remembers the process they went through when they started another phase of curriculum mapping:

> **Literacy Coach:** *At the beginning where it was like, oh let's just bring our science book and look at the topics in the science book, you know, and then...they sat down and determined what the state standards were and what the expectations are and then who was going to really focus in on a particular skill.*

In reflecting back over the school years, another literacy coach remembered her own development as a teacher, learning to score and analyze student work.

> **Literacy Coach:** *You know (laughter), we went from that [where we had never scored student work on a rubric] to looking at the rubric to actually like scoring each other's papers and seeing if we like scored them the right way. You know, and like talking about like what a four would look like; what a three would look like...*
>
> *What does a writing piece look like? And then also going back to the classroom and having the students work on their rubric. I mean, because like you said in the beginning, we never even saw it...So, yeah, that was huge.*

The teacher focus group also discussed the school's use of assessments and differences between their use and understanding of how to use assessments compared to other teachers. These perceptions align with the data on Reflective Dialogue from the 2007 CCSR survey where over 95% of the teachers reported that they shared and discussed student work with other teachers.

**Teacher 1:** *We were doing those self-assessments before the Board started the Learning First [assessments in 2005]. Learning First is the same thing. It is three times a year: fall, winter, spring. It is reading and it's math. And it's multiple choice and it's also an extended response in both subjects. It is exactly what we were doing, and all of a sudden [the district] started doing it. When we were doing it, I'm going to workshops, and people from other schools were like, Why do you do that? Nobody was doing it, nobody.*

**Teacher 2:** *Right.*

**Teacher 3:** *That may be. I don't know how many schools were involved with Partnership [READ], eight schools, in the beginning, less than that, but now citywide those Learning First assessments were really what we were doing years before.*

**Teacher 1:** *We are probably using them more effectively than other schools; like we have been analyzing that now.*

**Teacher 2:** *We were the pilot school [for the math benchmark assessment]. I remember going to workshops the first year we did Learning First; people hadn't done it, and I thought it was citywide and I learned at the workshop [that] there were just a few schools doing that as a pilot. Everyone didn't even use the Learning First when we first started. We were like really ahead of people.*

Teachers agreed that the use and analysis of assessment data was helpful for them to understand their students' learning needs, and it made a difference on their instructional approaches over time. They also stated that data discussions in schoolwide Gallery Walks were important and that people are more open now (2007) than they were before. When a question was posed about the importance of gallery walks, teachers responded in a variety of different ways:

**Teacher 1:** *I think so.*

**Teacher 2:** *It is challenging.*

**Teacher 3:** *…I think [the Gallery Walk] leads to some cohesiveness between the grade because the Gallery Walk in general…as bad as they were sometimes, you hear strategies, you hear struggles, [and] strengths. And you say to yourself, Well, our second grade is doing this and I want to do this and I wish fourth grade would do this. So even though we were already all kind of collaborating, to me the Gallery Walk—I [didn't] enjoy a Gallery Walk at all—it turned out to be good. They really are good things. Especially this year, we were all productive this year.*

**Teacher 4:** *The good thing about it is you are forced to share out. Whatever results you got or however you struggled or whatever you did that you are having trouble with you are forced to stand up there and share it with everybody and hear everybody else.*

**Teacher 5:** *And later you are going to go back to that teacher above you or below you and say, Hey, remember you said—*

**Teacher 6:** *I remember that definitely played a role in changing the culture in hearing how everyone was struggling because that first year we all thought we were alone and then it definitely took a while. People weren't as open as they are now but it definitely helps to hear that other people are struggling. And it was a way of acknowledging the mistakes you made. And you want to change it but you are not sure how and [so] you get some help. And I think we really do work together.*

During the discussion, another teacher added a different perspective on changes at the school. This teacher specifically addressed how teachers were expected to know what students were expected to learn and how that was different from previous years when teachers taught literacy by teaching one chapter after another from a test book. The school's focus on differentiating instruction is also addressed, stating how teachers shifted from teaching from podiums to teaching student-centered lessons in classrooms with tables for groups and learning centers.

**Teacher:** *To me everything changed when [the new administration] came. Every room in this school was just in straight rows instead of the way it [is now], and everybody was using textbooks from Chapter 1 to Chapter 20....Nobody ever heard of standards [-based] instruction throughout the school.*

*Everyone was just using [the textbooks], and the books are written for nationwide [use] so then—and then since there was no accountability, you could teach any topic that you wanted to teach....[The new administration] is the one that instituted [this change]. You were now forced to know the standards at your grade level. You were forced to put them in...their lesson plans.*

*A lot of people would complain, "Why do I have to rewrite that? I have the paper." But you had to write or type that. So you had to write out entire standards and...know what is expected of your students at your grade level to learn, not what is in the textbook that isn't related to whether you test or not. But you had to know the standards and you had to use the standards and incorporate them into your planning and that's what you used to pass it on.*

*Then came the big push with [differentiated] learning and everybody is [now]—you won't find a room without little tables—there were no centers here [before]. They were all teachers making student-centered type lessons because mostly the teacher—we had a lot of teachers [teaching] at the podiums [before].*

Teachers shared their perceptions of how their use of grade-level team meetings evolved. They spoke favorably about meeting with colleagues, having more time to communicate with one another, and sharing strategies. This conversation also aligns closely to CCSR data on Reflective Dialogue.

**Teacher:** *We shared strategies more, where before I might only hear what [other] grade [levels are] doing in a Gallery Walk or even other people in my cluster. And now in grade-level meetings we share actual strategies that we are using in our classrooms. So it is more time to communicate with people where I didn't have that before, so it is handing over more a little bit. Like [what was said before] things need to be worked on to improve it, but we were talking more and sharing strategies, not just how we were improving assessments, but just... different content and how that was working, and that was helpful.*

## Meeting Challenges

The data from literacy coaches and teachers show how they evolved in their use of an assessment or rubric to inform curriculum planning and teaching. For each school year, new challenges were presented by students, parents, teachers, administrators, Illinois State Board of Education, No Child Left Behind, or the area or district offices. The challenges from these forces helped to propel the school forward into other aspects of teaching and learning. One literacy coach reflected on one of those new challenges.

**Literacy Coach:** *Differentiation definitely came in later [2005 and 2006] when there was more emphasis put on, you know, having guided reading and working with students at their level and knowing where to bring them up from. There was more collaboration occurring and teachers working together and analyzing say a writing sample together. Like I'm going to look at your fourth-grade sample... we're going to exchange samples, and how would you rate this paper? You know, like where do you think the strength of this student lies and what would you do about it? And just having that conversation about student by student and learn how to like say analyze a writing piece, you know, because we weren't taught that either. It was like okay, well this looks good. Well, what are you looking at? What are the components in the rubric? That was a whole other thing, too.*

## Engaging Students

Over the years, students were directly involved in understanding the curriculum and expectations, and they also learned how to use a rubric to score their written work. Student engagement in the process was deliberate. Students were involved in the process after teachers developed student expectations for an eighth-grade graduate and student expectations that advanced in rigor from preschool to eighth grade. Student-friendly outcomes, otherwise known as "I cans," were explained and displayed in all classrooms. In addition, students learned to use rubrics to score their work and the work of their peers.

> **Literacy Coach:** *And also the fact that the "I cans" are visible and the children understand the "I cans," which is the student-friendly outcome. And they understand the expectations, so everyone is a part of the process. And I think...the issue [was] the teaching with the rubric and the child understanding, well, you can't get a three unless you have say an introduction in the details within your paper. And this is what a three looks like, and this is what a four looks like. And the kids were actually trading papers and they had their little mini rubric. And like...no I can't give you this because you didn't do such and such, and you have to do this to be on that part of the rubric. And you know, so it helped that the children were involved and understood the expectations, and we all learned about rubrics.*

One important stage in the Standards-Based Change Process is student engagement, where students know the expected outcomes, then own the learning outcomes by monitoring their progress using rubrics. Student engagement in these processes was important. However, significant teacher progress in the development of learning outcomes, assessments, and rubrics to assess student written work was essential prior to engaging students.

## Change in Focus for Curriculum Planning

The Standards-Based Change Process enabled teachers to maintain a continuum that advanced teaching and learning at the school. Teacher learning, both self-reported in CCSR surveys and in focus group comments, was continuous.

The sequence of curriculum planning activities and the changes in curriculum development over the years are illustrated in Figure 6.8 on the following page. During the first two years, South Loop focused on developing learning outcomes, with teachers engaged in developing assessments and rubrics to score student writing during the second year. The activities during the summer of 2004 are what one teacher previously coined as the "behind-the-scenes work." During this time, dedicated teams of teachers, literacy coaches, and administrators worked together to further develop systems and structures for programs and to further develop curriculum. This work took time. The curriculum development work involved a review of the learning outcomes, and revisions were made as needed to ensure that they were rigorous. By 2005, many teachers were using data and rubrics to guide curriculum planning. Again, teacher teams worked over the summer. During the summer of 2005, the focus in the curriculum shifted from developing reading, writing, and math outcomes to social science and science curriculum planning. One goal for this work, for example, was to embed reading comprehension and writing outcomes into the social science curriculum. After four years of work, during 2006, the norm was for teachers to use data to differentiate curriculum with the goal of meeting student learning needs. Student engagement in their learning also moved to a new level during 2006, where teachers involved students in scoring their writing by using rubrics.

**Figure 6.8. Change in Focus for Curriculum, 2003–2007**

| August 2002–June 2003 | August 2003–June 2004 | June and Summer 2004 | August 2004–June 2005 | August 2005–June 2006 |
|---|---|---|---|---|
| • Reading standards curriculum map—Working toward schoolwide coherence | • Reading standards curriculum map—Working toward schoolwide coherence<br>• Teachers collaboratively score student work using rubrics | • Reading standards curriculum map—Rigor across the curriculum further developed | • Assessments, data, and rubrics are utilized as road maps for curriculum planning | • Differentiated curriculum<br>• Guided reading<br>• Students score student work for self and peers using rubrics |

## A Professional Learning Community Sustains Change

South Loop grew and developed, becoming a professional learning community. As we saw in this chapter, this development did not happen overnight, yet at the same time, as one teacher noted, some aspects developed rather quickly. The foundation was the drive from the school administration for coherence, an approach that turned grade-level team meetings and professional development workshops into systems, structures, and routines that supported the work that was core for the school's development. As teachers developed their capacity in the use of assessments and assessment data, teachers better understood the needs of their students. This led to curriculum planning designed to meet the learning needs of their students. As a result of the consistent press for teachers' meetings and professional development workshops where plans were developed collaboratively for instruction, teachers learned to work together and to value these times together.

The growth in reflective dialogue, the willingness to assume collective responsibility, and the upward trend in teacher innovation increased teacher capacity. The sum of the parts became greater than the whole. South Loop reversed the trends and patterns that were embedded in its history, and as a result, students, teachers, administrators, and families benefited. The teachers and administration learned how to work together toward a common goal—increased student achievement—and as a result, a professional learning community developed. However, it is important to point out that as the community developed, students were strategically engaged in the process. The spirit of the professional learning community did not stop with the teachers.

One sign of the strength of a school's professional learning community is its ability to sustain change. As I mentioned previously, I am no longer the principal at South Loop, as I accepted a district-level position in June 2007. Since that time, the teachers and administration at South Loop, and Univerity of Illinois at Chicago's Partnership READ continue to collaborate and are moving the school forward. Upward trends for core school metrics continue, as student achievement and school enrollment have increased. In addition to these metrics, many others could be mentioned. However, one unusual event tells a more complete story.

In October 2008, the Chicago Board of Education voted at its meeting to open a new school, one that replicates South Loop. An article titled "Cloning South Loop School," published in *The Chicago Journal*, a local neighborhood paper, reports one perspective on this event. The editor states that, "a new elementary school based on the *South Loop Way* has the go-ahead to open next fall following an affirmative vote by the Board of Education at its October meeting" (Maidenberg 2008). Asked what the board vote meant, spokesman Malon Edwards said CPS was impressed with operations at South Loop School. Test scores at the school are rising. In 2005, for example, 58% of third graders were meeting or exceeding state reading standards. That number increased to more than 82 percent last year. Similar gains were made in other grades. Malon went on to describe satisfaction among board members and parents, taking particular note that South Loop didn't start off the way it is now. Maidenberg also interviewed Melissa Mister, principal at the new school, who explained that the "South Loop Way" means "collective responsibility" for student achievement. Mister explained, "It's used to describe the whole program, where there's collective responsibility for results, where everyone's working collaboratively to make sure students' outcomes are continuously improving."

The core systems, structures, and routines continue, with teams of teachers at the core of the work. Now this work expands to the South Shore Fine Arts Academy. A professional learning community sustains change. The South Loop Professional Learning Community not only sustained change—it allowed change to flourish.

> "If professional learning communities offer our best hope for school improvement, a critical question facing educators is this: How can we develop school cultures that reflect the ideals and practices of professional learning communities?"
> —Eaker and Keating (2008, 15)

## Reflection: Thinking About Teaching and Learning

1. From the chapter, select one quotation that best represents your perspective about professional learning communities—what they are, how they work, and what they offer teachers. Share your observations about the quotation with colleagues, or jot down some thoughts in your professional learning journal.

2. Refer to the survey items for Reflective Dialogue (Figure 6.2, p. 120), Collective Responsibility (Figure 6.3, p. 123), and Innovation (Figure 6.5, p. 128). How would you respond to the items in each survey? Do you think that your responses and those of colleagues would be similar? What value do you think such data offer a faculty in efforts to improve teaching and learning?

3. Look back at the remarks of the literacy coaches and teachers (pp. 131–137). What insights into a professional learning community do these remarks offer?

4. The "South Loop Way" means "collective responsibility" for student achievement (see p. 141). What thoughts do you have about implementing the "South Loop Way" in other schools?

# Chapter 7

# Lessons Learned About School Change

The description of school change in this book is drawn from my case study of South Loop Elementary School in Chicago where I served as principal. The study provided an in-depth look at the complexity of how this school achieved change in its culture and in its approach to curriculum and instruction from August 2002 to June 2007. My experience at South Loop, together with what I knew about school improvement at the time I joined the school's faculty, told me that improving learning outcomes in the school would require not simply implementing a different literacy curriculum but would also require that the school as a whole undergo considerable change in how it conducted its business. This was once a high-need urban school with multiple issues—from significant challenges in the school culture to significant student misbehavior, to rapid principal turnover, to conflicts within the school's Local School Council that hires and fires principals. A new literacy curriculum would not by itself be likely to succeed in that environment. The school would have to make significant changes as a culture, and at the same time seek to make all due haste in improving student learning outcomes. I strongly suspected that the two—school culture and student achievement—were linked, but at the outset I did not know exactly how to link them. As a result of conducting the case study, I now have better understanding and appreciation of the connections between teacher learning and student achievement.

## Insights from Conducting a Case Study

As the overview of the school's history illustrates (see Chapter 1), significant changes took place at South Loop over a relatively short period. While it is important to see that a high-need urban school with a resistant and entrenched culture changed, it is equally important to see how this change happened. The case study gave me the opportunity to reflect on my experiences at South Loop and to gain perspective that is difficult to attain when one is involved in the everyday operations of a school. This reflection, combined with analyses of data about the school, provided insights into the positive impact of professional development that is embedded in the work of the school—ongoing formative assessments, interpretation of the assessment data, teacher dialogue and discussion about the use of data to shape instruction, and standards-based curriculum. These actions are important elements in a professional learning community, but they must be accompanied by structural and organizational changes that foster collegial and collaborative effort in an environment that engenders trust and respect among all the stakeholders—school leadership, teachers, students, and community. In describing professional learning communities, Fullan observed that "terms travel easily...but the underlying concepts do not" (2005, 67). Saying the school is a "professional learning community" is one thing; actually transforming it to function as such an entity requires much more than the use of the label. Achieving the transformation requires a focal point—at South Loop that point was the use of standardized and formative assessments in an effort to improve student learning in literacy. Embedded in that focus are factors that influence the intended outcome of improved student learning through improved classroom instruction: systems and structures to support the use of assessments and assessment data, the role of assessments and assessment data in teacher meetings and professional development sessions, and the impact of assessment data on curriculum planning. Results in each of these areas have been examined in previous chapters of this book.

There were setbacks and challenges to the reform work that took place at South Loop. The school resided in a complicated environment with challenging circumstances. Throughout the time of the study—2003 through 2007—changes occurred in school personnel and school policies. Many of these changes were difficult for teachers, staff, school administration, parents, and students—and there was resistance. However, as the study illustrates, as new systems and structures became routines and student achievement improved, more and more members of the school community chose to work together on the goals the South Loop leadership team defined.

Using data in decision making is critical to the types of changes needed in urban schools like South Loop. When data is used for school improvement, the activities must be constructive and related to practice so that teachers can trust that the data will not be used against them. The cultural shift that this requires includes commitment to the belief that teacher learning can improve student learning and that professional learning communities support and foster teacher learning.

## A Comprehensive Framework for Implementing School Change

While the process of Standards-Based Change provided a list of tasks to accomplish for curricular work, at the outset the school leadership team did not have a framework that they owned to guide its work. We soon learned the value of a framework, a theory of action, to guide our efforts and to help teachers better understand how what was being asked of them fit into the big picture. Over the course of the implementation of formative assessments to drive teaching and learning, the leadership team developed a model that we used to guide the continuous improvement cycle that teachers engaged in throughout the year. This model was teacher-centered; that is, it provided a roadmap that made clear the role of the teacher in each step of the process. The model, presented in Figure 7.1 (on the following page), provides a comprehensive perspective of the key structures that were critical to support the work that teachers were engaged in. The structures and activities shown in this model were essential to the development of the South Loop learning community and for the school's improvement in its

> "...the question is whether other school systems, operating in an environment of increased attention to student performance and quality of instruction, will discover that they need to learn not just different ways of doing things, but very different ways of thinking about the purpose of their work, and the skills and knowledge that go with those purposes."
> —Elmore (2002, 35)

collaborations around curriculum, instruction, and assessment.

**Figure 7.1. Focused and Continuous Improvement Cycle**

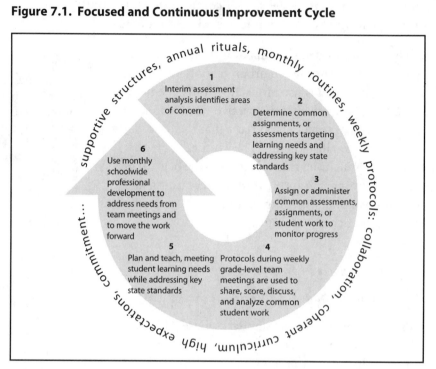

From the beginning, a coherent plan—one that aligned the school's structures and routines with the school's professional development plan and with work expectations for teachers—could have provided a better road map for the work that was ahead. As the circle on the outside of the model illustrates, the work for school teams must be supported by structures—annual rituals, monthly routines, and weekly protocols during team meetings. Each of these structures is grounded in high expectations for the quality of teacher professionalism, support for teacher collaboration, and reflective dialogue on teaching and learning. The links and interconnectedness among the supportive structures of regularly scheduled team meetings, schoolwide professional development, and the focused work that districts and school leadership teams ask of their teachers is critical. Data demonstrate that by making connections among the degree of rigor expected of the student work, the focus for weekly grade-level team meetings, and teacher professional development workshops, this reform has the potential to accelerate the quality of teacher conversations on teaching and learning. Data also demonstrate that this approach has the potential to accelerate school change, providing educators the opportunity to address student learning needs today, rather than waiting several years for a reform to take hold.

## Need for a Coherent Plan

The structured use of standardized and formative assessments led to changes in conversations and curriculum planning around student learning. While this process was critical to the success of South Loop, reflection on what and how events transpired indicated to me that the model used initially, "Utilizing Ongoing Formative Assessments" (Figure 7.2 below), can be improved.

**Figure 7.2. Utilizing Ongoing Formative Assessments**

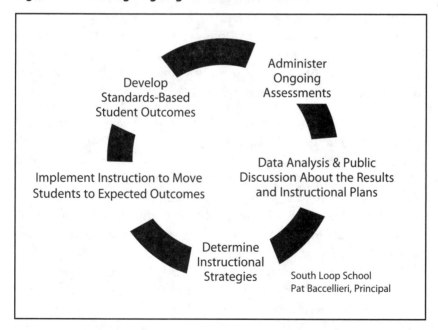

In its early form, this model didn't include structures and routines to support assessment and curriculum work because these were just being developed. The model (Figure 7.2) centered on assessments and their use, but lacked structural details that would have helped teachers to understand the whole picture. The model needed refinement to better illustrate the importance of establishing the structures and routines that can bring coherence to the work at the school. Such elements were critical to the successes achieved over the years at South Loop. By developing this model and making it available, districts and schools interested in making change can consider how this model could support work that they are engaged in to move their school communities forward. This could help bring coherence to the work, rather than develop the framework along the way as we did at South Loop. Clarity about the framework can possibly contribute to smoother advances toward change. For example, South Loop data demonstrate that the interconnectedness among the improvement agenda the school leadership team established for the year, the work of the literacy coaches, expectations for what took place in grade-level team meetings, and schoolwide professional development plans improved over the course of this study. However, it took three years for those seemingly separate activities to meld.

It is reasonable to suppose that the development of the school learning community could have been a little smoother for all involved had a comprehensive plan integrating these separate activities been in place at the start of 2003. Granted, there were many factors to consider: competing needs to be addressed, time constraints, and the considerably low levels of trust, coherence, and innovation. Data also demonstrate that the literacy coaches needed more support in the beginning as they worked to facilitate grade-level team meetings and to manage some of the challenges that came when new expectations were put into place for teachers. Teachers also expressed frustration about the amount of time they were able to use during grade-level team meetings to review student writing and other assessment data and to plan curriculum. While teachers noted that eventually more time was made available for them during grade-level team meetings, had this change occurred earlier in South Loop's reform, some teachers would have welcomed it.

At the same time, it is useful to acknowledge that there are different perspectives on the extent to which a framework can be implemented. Finding one's own way can be an important element of the professional learning community. However, greater continuity in the process could have been improved early on in the reform, and the press to accomplish the new work could have been implemented in a more coherent fashion. In other words, there are limits to the "do-it-yourself" model, or the "building-the-plane-while-flying-it" approach. Nonetheless, there are advantages to having at least some pieces in place or a framework to begin working from rather than doing everything from scratch. Undoubtedly, each school must be prepared to adjust a framework to address and accommodate circumstances unique to its situation.

## Protocols for Meetings

Along with a coherent plan from the beginning, the use of protocols to guide and support grade-level team meetings would have provided routines and structures for these meetings. Aside from support from school administration and the university partner to develop a meeting agenda to help the facilitator lead the meetings, there is a demonstrated need for protocols and other instruments to help schools conduct productive meetings, therefore reducing the need for each school to figure this out on its own. A protocol is a guide through the process of professional judgment and provides clear steps to accomplish a task. Once the teachers, literacy coaches, and administrators agree on the steps for how a meeting will be conducted or how student writing will be analyzed, then each time teacher teams meet, the protocol can be followed.

A protocol can be relatively basic or complex. In many ways, the guide to conducting a Gallery Walk (see Figure 5.3, p. 103) can be considered a protocol. Protocols provide structured ways for teams to work together and provide greater equity for peer-to-peer engagement and peer-to-administrator interaction. Examples of such protocols are readily available in the fields of medicine and education.

The steps in Figure 7.1 (p. 146) provide some clues to protocols that can facilitate a school's use of assessments and data to increase the quality and rigor of student written work. Note that the terminology in this model is generic, rather than specific to how South Loop used the cycle of improvement. Examples of protocols associated with each of the steps are described here:

- **Step 1:** Multiple sources of data collected over time provide data demonstrating areas of concern and success.

- **Steps 2 and 3:** Curriculum-embedded assignments and formative assessments are used. South Loop teachers developed common formative assessments for each grade level and administered them three times a year. Improving the quality of the assessments was a focus for the teachers over time. As a result, the level of rigor for the assessments increased. While this approach worked for the school on several different levels, there are other ways to accomplish the same end. For example, a district or school could use a Kindergarten through eighth or twelfth grade coherent curriculum to anchor this work. The curriculum would need to be vetted to ensure that the level of rigor at each grade level is appropriate and that the curriculum is grounded in the state learning standards. Next, a district or school team could use student achievement data to determine the areas of focus—for example, reading comprehension, writing, fluency, math problem solving, and so on. From there, the teams identify key benchmarks that are critical for students to learn in the focus area. Teams could next develop or identify writing prompts, key assignments, or parts of assignments from the curriculum that are equal to the level of rigor expected by the benchmarks.

- **Step 4:** Assignments or common student work products are the focus for grade-level meetings. Using samples of student work that vary in quality, teachers collaboratively examine the student materials. They work in teams to review the student work against specific learning objectives or criteria presented in the form of a rubric. The aim in this phase is for teams to come to a consensus on the level of rigor for the student work samples, agreeing on those that are below, meeting, or exceeding the state standards. During this step, teachers have the opportunity to discuss the specific criteria that distinguish each student work product from the next. Data demonstrate that teacher learning at this phase of the cycle led to a clearer understanding of what was critical for students to know and be able to do, providing teachers with a clearer understanding of where to focus the curriculum.

- **Step 5:** Teachers are involved in planning, focusing curriculum and instruction designed to move students to expected outcomes. They draw on data results to inform instructional decisions.

- **Step 6:** This step occurs monthly, or when the district or school has workshops scheduled for professional development. These workshops should be designed to support teacher teams as they strive to focus teaching and learning to meet the learning needs of their students. These workshops must also push teachers to engage in the next level of the work that the leadership team determines is critical to move the school community forward toward their vision and mission.

The value of a coherent plan cannot be underestimated. The plan provides transparency, which is necessary to avoid the second-guessing and pushback that sometimes occur with efforts to implement change. In addition, the plan provides clarity of purpose, predictability about expectations, and evidence that the work teachers are called upon to accomplish is related to what goes on in the classroom.

"Learning in context has the greatest potential payoff because it is more specific, situational, and social (it develops shared and collective knowledge and commitments). This kind of learning is designed to improve the organization *and* its social and moral context. Learning in context also establishes conditions conducive to continual development, including opportunities to learn from others on the job, the daily fostering of current and future leaders, the selective retention of good ideas and best practices, and the explicit monitoring of performance."
—Fullan (2005, 67)

## Final Thoughts

While serving as the principal at South Loop Elementary School, I was in the habit of processing the day's events every evening, reviewing what occurred, considering what I could have done differently, and also working to develop solutions to puzzling dilemmas. I also took stock every year in December and January, reflecting on the work that had taken place over the course of a year. I remember when I was reflecting on my second year at South Loop, I was feeling the weight of school change on my shoulders. And it dawned on me—the sign that we were making progress was not that we didn't have problems, but I realized that I was focused on different ones. This gave me a sense of hope; change was taking place.

Conducting this study provided me the opportunity to look at the practices put in place at South Loop over five years from the inside-out and the outside-in. Exploring professional development plans and grade-level team meeting minutes and reading teacher and literacy coach memories from the focus groups provided a new lens into South Loop that I never had before. The data from the Chicago Consortium on School Research were also very helpful to me. Like the grade-level team meetings, these survey results were records of how teachers perceived their work while they were engaged in it. I also remember my decision to conduct the survey during the spring of my first year at South Loop in 2003. I was pretty sure that I knew what the outcome of the survey would be, but I also knew that I had to face the brutal facts and figure out how to move the school forward. Exploring data from 2003 and 2007 confirmed for me that teachers now have better working relationships and are thriving in their work, and that students and families are benefiting.

It is clear to me how important it is to implement systems and structures within the school day and professional development plans so that teachers have the opportunity to work together. Systems like common grade-level team meetings and schoolwide events where teachers formally presented common assessments, the achievement data of their students, and their plan to address the learning needs of their students became the core of the work at the school. These provided opportunities for continuous cycles of assessments and professionally led discussions, ending with curriculum planning. As a result, teachers learned how to engage with one another, looked at and discussed common assessments or assignments that their students completed, and then collaboratively planned how to address the learning needs of their students. South Loop is a different place today than it was in 2002. Conducting this case study helped me better understand what mattered most.

As a result, this study helps me in my current administrative responsibilities. As a district administrator, I currently support principals and their teams, working collaboratively to make school improvements in high-need urban schools. I know that we can reverse the trends of student underachievement. I also know that we need teams of teachers, instructional coaches, and administrators working side by side with students and their families to bring change to our schools. It affirms for me the importance of developing systems and structures that support teacher collaboration, where teachers, instructional coaches, coordinators, and administrators come together for a common purpose—increasing the quality of student achievement. This study also affirms for me the importance of a sustained focus over time, one that uses common assessments and assessment data with the aim of understanding what strategies students need in their classrooms or grade levels to increase their achievement. Furthermore, it affirms for me the importance in the belief that all involved in working in a school can pull together to become a professional learning community. Without a doubt, what occurred at South Loop was hard work, but undoubtedly, the systems and structures put in place serve as a foundation for the school. As a result, the South Loop professional learning community became a force that changed its circumstances and its history.

> "We cannot expect teachers to create a vigorous community of learners among students if they have no parallel community to nourish themselves."
> —Sarason (1990, 49)

## Reflection: Thinking About Teaching and Learning

1. From the chapter, select one quotation that best represents your perspective of what this case study of South Loop Elementary School offers educators who desire to improve teaching and learning. Share your observations about the quotation with colleagues, or jot down some thoughts in your professional learning journal.

2. "Conducting this case study helped me better understand what mattered most" (p. 153). In what ways has the story of South Loop Elementary School affected your thinking about school change?

3. What features of this case study would you choose as guideposts to facilitate a process of change within your school? Compare your choices with colleagues who have also read this book.

## Chapter 3

### Appendix 3.1. NAEP Reading Achievement Level Policy Definitions (2001–Present)

| Achievement Level | Definition |
| --- | --- |
| Basic | **Partial mastery** of prerequisite knowledge and skills that are fundamental for proficient work at each grade. |
| Proficient | **Solid academic performance** for each grade assessed. Students reaching this level have demonstrated competency over challenging subject matter, including subject-matter knowledge, application of such knowledge to real-world situations, and analytical skills appropriate to the subject matter. |
| Advanced | **Superior performance**. |

Source: National Center for Education Statistics (n.d.). *Reading: The NAEP reading achievement levels.*
**http://nces.ed.gov/nationsreportcard/reading/achieveall.asp**

## Appendix 3.2. NAEP Reading Achievement Levels Definitions

The Federal No Child Left Behind (NCLB) Act of 2002 is one of the attempts legislators made to increase student academic achievement. The law required revisions to NAEP achievement levels, which are now designed to define and measure student achievement in fourth, eighth and twelfth grades in all subjects assessed by NAEP. The results are intended to show what students know and what they are able to do. For each of the grades assessed, NAEP has developed a scale score that corresponds to each level of proficiency in reading. In addition, the NCLB Act holds states accountable to move all students to scoring at the proficient level on state standardized tests by the 2014 school year. NCLB mandates that each state will test all elementary level students in grades three through eight each year in reading and math, and also test a sample of students in fourth and eighth grades every other year in the once optional NAEP assessments. NAEP data will provide for cross-state comparisons.

Definitions of the *Basic, Proficient,* and *Advanced* achievement levels for grades four and eight are presented. The achievement levels are cumulative. Therefore, students performing at the *Proficient* level also display the competencies associated with the *Basic* level, and students at the *Advanced* level also demonstrate the skills and knowledge associated with both the *Basic* and the *Proficient* levels. For each achievement level listed, the scale score that corresponds to the beginning of that level is shown in parentheses.

## Appendix 3.2. NAEP Reading Achievement Levels Definitions (cont.)

### Grade 4

| Achievement Level | Definition |
|---|---|
| Basic (208) | Fourth-grade students performing at the *Basic* level should demonstrate an understanding of the overall meaning of what they read. When reading text appropriate for fourth-graders, they should be able to make relatively obvious connections between the text and their own experiences and extend the ideas in the text by making simple inferences. |
| Proficient (238) | Fourth-grade students performing at the *Proficient* level should be able to demonstrate an overall understanding of the text, providing inferential as well as literal information. When reading text appropriate to fourth grade, they should be able to extend the ideas in the text by making inferences, drawing conclusions, and making connections to their own experiences. The connection between the text and what the student infers should be clear. |
| Advanced (268) | Fourth-grade students performing at the *Advanced* level should be able to generalize about topics in the reading selection and demonstrate an awareness of how authors compose and use literary devices. When reading text appropriate to fourth grade, they should be able to judge text critically and, in general, to give thorough answers that indicate careful thought. |

Sources: National Center for Education Statistics. (n.d.). *Reading: The NAEP reading achievement levels.* http://nces.ed.gov/nationsreportcard/reading/achieveall.asp;National Center for Education Statistics. (n.d.). *Reading: The status of achievement levels.*; National Center for Education Statistics. (n.d.). *State profiles: Achievement levels for reading, national public.*

## Appendix 3.2. NAEP Reading Achievement Levels Definitions (cont.)

### Grade 8

| Achievement Level | Definition |
|---|---|
| Basic (243) | Eighth-grade students performing at the *Basic* level should demonstrate a literal understanding of what they read and be able to make some interpretations. When reading text appropriate to eighth grade, they should be able to identify specific aspects of the text that reflect overall meaning, extend the ideas in the text by making simple inferences, recognize and relate interpretations and connections among ideas in the text to personal experience, and draw conclusions based on the text. |
| Proficient (281) | Eighth-grade students performing at the *Proficient* level should be able to show an overall understanding of the text, including inferential as well as literal information. When reading text appropriate to eighth grade, they should be able to extend the ideas in the text by making clear inferences from it, by drawing conclusions, and by making connections to their own experiences—including other reading experiences. Proficient eighth-graders should be able to identify some of the devices authors use in composing text. |
| Advanced (323) | Eighth-grade students performing at the *Advanced* level should be able to describe the more abstract themes and ideas of the overall text. When reading text appropriate to eighth grade, they should be able to analyze both meaning and form and support their analyses explicitly with examples from the text; they should be able to extend text information by relating it to their experiences and to world events. At this level, student responses should be thorough, thoughtful, and extensive. |

Sources: National Center for Education Statistics. (n.d.). *Reading: The NAEP reading achievement levels.* http://nces.ed.gov/nationsreportcard/reading/achieveall.asp;National Center for Education Statistics. (n.d.). *Reading: The status of achievement levels.*; National Center for Education Statistics. (n.d.). *State profiles: Achievement levels for reading, national public.*

**Appendix 3.3. Expectations for all Teachers and Staff at South Loop Elementary School—Local Criteria for Teacher Evaluation, July 1, 2006–June 30, 2007**

### Provide a yearlong curriculum outline that includes:

- using standards-based assessments to inform and shape instruction

- using weekly and long-range outcome and standards-based lesson plans

- integrating the Chicago Reading Initiative into all curriculum

- using visible standards-driven "I can" statements daily

- providing differentiated instruction to meet individual student learning needs

- providing the least-restrictive environment for all students

- integrating learning centers into daily lessons and practices

- developing projects and assignments that integrate Social Science, Language Arts, Math, Science, Technology, Health and Fitness, and Fine Arts with the school's standards-based outcomes

- providing monthly classroom newsletters that clearly articulate information about student achievement, outcomes, and the curriculum

- actively participating in all aspects of the standards-based process, including professional development and curriculum development

- actively participating in leading one or two schoolwide events

- actively supporting and implementing PBIS: The South Loop Way

- conducting a minimum of one staff development presentation to the staff or a workshop for parents

- keeping a log of parent contacts; this includes all positive or negative telephone, written, and face-to-face contacts

- collaborating with teachers by actively engaging in peer coaching during weekly grade-level meetings and reviewing student work

- maintaining a minimum 95% attendance and promptness rate

- actively participating and demonstrating leadership in schoolwide initiatives, programs, and processes

- using at least three field trips to enhance the educational program

- presenting a positive attitude during the day, especially when you are requested to assist with an assignment or task

- being committed to work as a team in the many ways we are organized

- encouraging parent involvement and fully utilizing classroom parent volunteers

**Expectations for all teachers and staff at South Loop Elementary School:**

- attending a minimum of two Local School Council (LSC) meetings throughout the year

- participating in report card pickup and at least two open house events, one in September and one during the second semester

*Chapter 4*

## Appendix 4.1.  South Loop Elementary School, Area 9, District 299 (Chicago Public Schools)

**ISAT Composite Achievement Test Results (ISAT Overtime, 2007)**

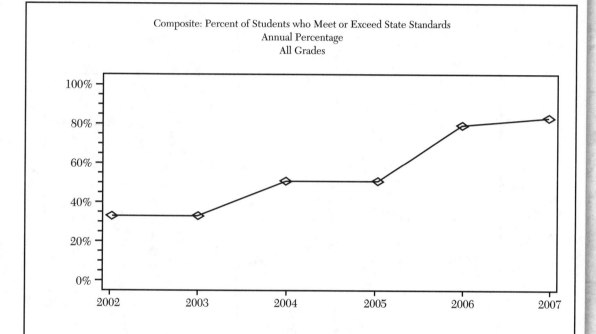

Composite: Percent of Students who Meet or Exceed State Standards
Annual Percentage
All Grades

City, Area, and School Summary

| | 2002 | | 2003 | | 2004 | | 2005 | | 2006 | | 2007 | |
|---|---|---|---|---|---|---|---|---|---|---|---|---|
| | N | % | N | % | N | % | N | % | N | % | N | % |
| City | 242,645 | 41.1% | 246,906 | 43.0% | 230,764 | 47.0% | 229,453 | 47.3% | 395,771 | 61.8% | 382,221 | 64.1% |
| Area | 9,993 | 46.6% | 10,175 | 46.0% | 9,163 | 53.6% | 9,089 | 54.4% | 15,720 | 68.0% | 14,959 | 69.8% |
| School | 336 | 32.4% | 283 | 32.5% | 261 | 51.3% | 255 | 51.0% | 438 | 80.1% | 507 | 83.4% |

*Chapter 4 (cont.)*

## Appendix 4.2. South Loop Elementary School, Area 9, District 299 (Chicago Public Schools)

**ISAT Reading Achievement Test Results (ISAT Overtime, 2007)**

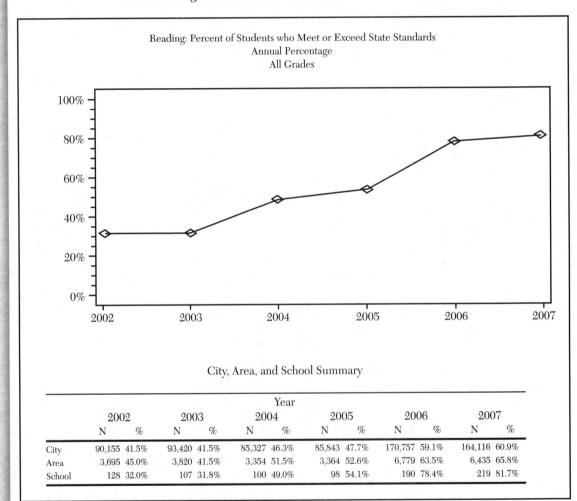

Reading: Percent of Students who Meet or Exceed State Standards
Annual Percentage
All Grades

City, Area, and School Summary

| | 2002 | | 2003 | | 2004 | | 2005 | | 2006 | | 2007 | |
|---|---|---|---|---|---|---|---|---|---|---|---|---|
| | N | % | N | % | N | % | N | % | N | % | N | % |
| City | 90,155 | 41.5% | 93,420 | 41.5% | 85,327 | 46.3% | 85,843 | 47.7% | 170,757 | 59.1% | 164,116 | 60.9% |
| Area | 3,695 | 45.0% | 3,820 | 41.5% | 3,354 | 51.5% | 3,364 | 52.6% | 6,779 | 63.5% | 6,435 | 65.8% |
| School | 128 | 32.0% | 107 | 31.8% | 100 | 49.0% | 98 | 54.1% | 190 | 78.4% | 219 | 81.7% |

## Appendix 4.3. South Loop Elementary School, Area 9, District 299 (Chicago Public Schools)

### ISAT Composite Achievement Test Results, Free and Reduced Lunch (ISAT Overtime, 2007)

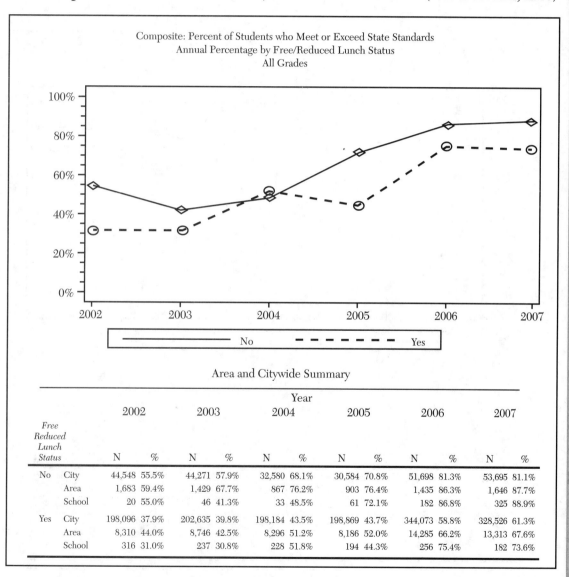

Composite: Percent of Students who Meet or Exceed State Standards
Annual Percentage by Free/Reduced Lunch Status
All Grades

Area and Citywide Summary

| Free Reduced Lunch Status | | 2002 | | 2003 | | 2004 | | 2005 | | 2006 | | 2007 | |
|---|---|---|---|---|---|---|---|---|---|---|---|---|---|
| | | N | % | N | % | N | % | N | % | N | % | N | % |
| No | City | 44,548 | 55.5% | 44,271 | 57.9% | 32,580 | 68.1% | 30,584 | 70.8% | 51,698 | 81.3% | 53,695 | 81.1% |
| | Area | 1,683 | 59.4% | 1,429 | 67.7% | 867 | 76.2% | 903 | 76.4% | 1,435 | 86.3% | 1,646 | 87.7% |
| | School | 20 | 55.0% | 46 | 41.3% | 33 | 48.5% | 61 | 72.1% | 182 | 86.8% | 325 | 88.9% |
| Yes | City | 198,096 | 37.9% | 202,635 | 39.8% | 198,184 | 43.5% | 198,869 | 43.7% | 344,073 | 58.8% | 328,526 | 61.3% |
| | Area | 8,310 | 44.0% | 8,746 | 42.5% | 8,296 | 51.2% | 8,186 | 52.0% | 14,285 | 66.2% | 13,313 | 67.6% |
| | School | 316 | 31.0% | 237 | 30.8% | 228 | 51.8% | 194 | 44.3% | 256 | 75.4% | 182 | 73.6% |

*Chapter 4 (cont.)*

## Appendix 4.4. South Loop Elementary School, Area 9, District 299 (Chicago Public Schools)

**ISAT Reading Achievement Test Results, Free and Reduced Lunch (ISAT Overtime, 2007)**

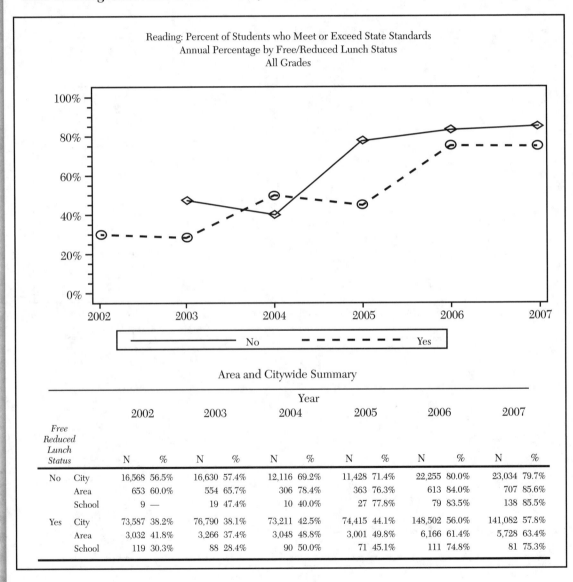

Reading: Percent of Students who Meet or Exceed State Standards
Annual Percentage by Free/Reduced Lunch Status
All Grades

Area and Citywide Summary

| Free Reduced Lunch Status | | 2002 N | 2002 % | 2003 N | 2003 % | 2004 N | 2004 % | 2005 N | 2005 % | 2006 N | 2006 % | 2007 N | 2007 % |
|---|---|---|---|---|---|---|---|---|---|---|---|---|---|
| No | City | 16,568 | 56.5% | 16,630 | 57.4% | 12,116 | 69.2% | 11,428 | 71.4% | 22,255 | 80.0% | 23,034 | 79.7% |
| | Area | 653 | 60.0% | 554 | 65.7% | 306 | 78.4% | 363 | 76.3% | 613 | 84.0% | 707 | 85.6% |
| | School | 9 | — | 19 | 47.4% | 10 | 40.0% | 27 | 77.8% | 79 | 83.5% | 138 | 85.5% |
| Yes | City | 73,587 | 38.2% | 76,790 | 38.1% | 73,211 | 42.5% | 74,415 | 44.1% | 148,502 | 56.0% | 141,082 | 57.8% |
| | Area | 3,032 | 41.8% | 3,266 | 37.4% | 3,048 | 48.8% | 3,001 | 49.8% | 6,166 | 61.4% | 5,728 | 63.4% |
| | School | 119 | 30.3% | 88 | 28.4% | 90 | 50.0% | 71 | 45.1% | 111 | 74.8% | 81 | 75.3% |

## Appendix 4.5. Program Coherence 2003. South Loop Elementary School Survey Report.

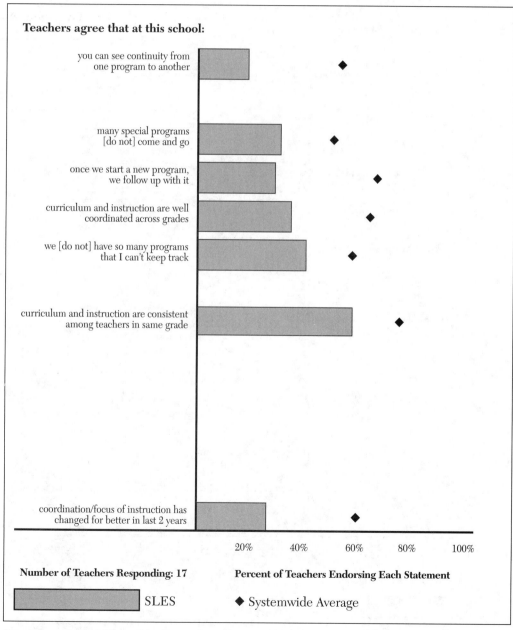

**Teachers agree that at this school:**

- you can see continuity from one program to another
- many special programs [do not] come and go
- once we start a new program, we follow up with it
- curriculum and instruction are well coordinated across grades
- we [do not] have so many programs that I can't keep track
- curriculum and instruction are consistent among teachers in same grade
- coordination/focus of instruction has changed for better in last 2 years

20%  40%  60%  80%  100%

**Number of Teachers Responding: 17**    **Percent of Teachers Endorsing Each Statement**

SLES    ◆ Systemwide Average

Source: Consortium on Chicago School Research, 2003.

## Appendix 4.6. Program Coherence 2007. South Loop Elementary School Survey Report.

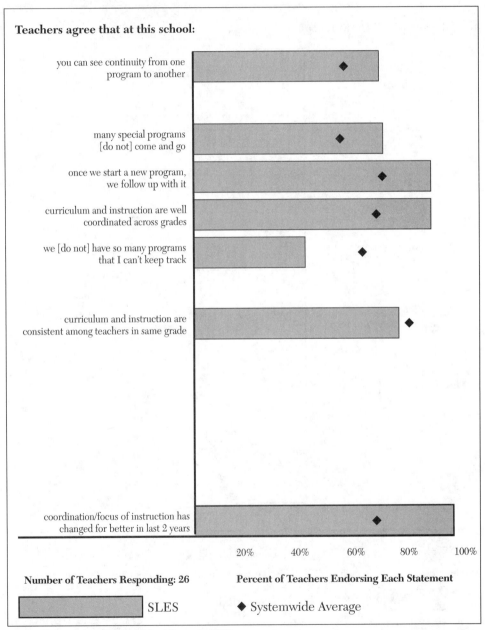

**Teachers agree that at this school:**

- you can see continuity from one program to another
- many special programs [do not] come and go
- once we start a new program, we follow up with it
- curriculum and instruction are well coordinated across grades
- we [do not] have so many programs that I can't keep track
- curriculum and instruction are consistent among teachers in same grade
- coordination/focus of instruction has changed for better in last 2 years

20%  40%  60%  80%  100%

**Number of Teachers Responding: 26**          **Percent of Teachers Endorsing Each Statement**

SLES          ◆ Systemwide Average

Source: Consortium on Chicago School Research, 2007.

*Chapter 5*

## Appendix 5.1  Sample Grade-Level Team Minutes School Year 2005

| Date | Grade Levels | Agenda Item(s) | Discussion | Actions to be completed |
|---|---|---|---|---|
| 01/05/05 | 2, 3 | Assessment Schedule | • Distributed and explained Mid-Year Assessment Schedule (on pink paper). | |
| 01/02/05 | 4, 5, 6 | Gallery Walk Criteria | • Discussed criteria for Gallery Walk (1/28) and Rubric for Curriculum Guide; Did a step-by-step review of what needs to be included in the Curriculum Guide.<br>• Discussed 5-min. report that will be given by each grade level (1/28).<br>• Received Extended Response for Reading strategy to use with class. | |
| 01/05/05 | 7, 8 | Assessment Schedule | • Discussed Mid-Year Assessment schedule.<br>• Began discussion about ISATs and how to best prepare students.<br>• Teachers reviewed the Comprehension assessments and made changes.<br>• Assessments to be distributed Friday (start on Monday). | |
| 01/05/05 | 3, 4, 5 | Assessment Schedules | • Schedules were distributed so teachers know which area to assess on which day. | |
| 01/06/05 | K, 1 | | • Final review of benchmark assessment information.<br>• Kindergarten handed in End-of-Year "I cans."<br>• Literacy Coach gave teachers all fluency materials. | |
| 01/06/05 | 2, 3 | | • Reviewed administration of fluency assessments<br>• Looked at "I cans" for each end of year. | • Teachers write "I cans" (1/12)<br>• Administer assessments (1/14)<br>• Grade assessments (1/21) |

## Appendix 5.1  Sample Grade-Level Team Minutes School Year 2005 *(cont.)*

| Date | Grade Levels | Agenda Item(s) | Discussion | Actions to be completed |
|---|---|---|---|---|
| 01/06/05 | 4, 5, 6 | | • No official meeting due to lack of subs; Teachers met one on one with Ms. Carter to review grade-level comprehension assessments.<br>• All fluency passages were discussed, distributed, and reviewed for proper scoring.<br>• All other assessments will be distributed tomorrow. | • Mid-Year Assessments by Grade Level Teachers (1/10–1/15) |
| 01/06/05 | 7, 8 | Fluency Assessments | • Fluency assessments were distributed to teachers and scoring was reviewed; Testing will start Monday; All other assessments will be given out tomorrow.<br>• ISAT subjects were reviewed to clarify what is tested for grades 7 and 8; Teachers discussed how to plan instruction and grouping of students; Preparation will start with lessons at the start of the new quarter. | • Mid-Year Assessments (1/10–1/15) |
| 01/13/05 | K, 1 | | • Literacy Coach handed out "I can" statements.<br>• Teachers reviewed assessments and individual scoring. | |
| 01/12/05 | 7, 8 | Gallery Walk | • Jan. 28th Gallery Walk memo was distributed to describe upcoming event; Teachers will be presenting midyear data results and instruction. Curriculum Guides will be reviewed on this day; Rubric was distributed to teachers and discussed.<br>• ISAT extended response has become a focus of instruction; Sample template/strategy was distributed to help teachers teach this lesson; One teacher discussed what is expected for a "4" for the math and how it is similar to writing. | Items assigned to teachers:<br>• Gallery Walk Presentation (1/28)<br>• Curriculum Guide (1/28)<br>• Assessment data due (1/21) |

## Appendix 5.1  Sample Grade-Level Team Minutes School Year 2005 (*cont.*)

| Date | Grade Levels | Agenda Item(s) | Discussion | Actions to be completed |
|---|---|---|---|---|
| 01/13/05 | 4, 5, 6 | Collaborative Scoring | • Collaborative scoring began and the comprehension rubrics were reviewed; Teachers will stay after school to continue to score. | • Scoring complete and data submitted (1/21) |
| 01/12/05 | K, 1 | | • "I can" statements are typed and can be put in binder.<br>• Literacy Coach went over the memo/rubric/guidelines for the Gallery Walk on 1/28.<br>• There are three Thursdays for Professional Development 3:00–5:00 p.m. (Jan. 13, Jan. 20, and Jan. 27). | • Literacy Coach will copy math/writing rubrics (1/14)<br>• Final procedure for K-Fluency (1/14)<br>• Copies of graphs to teachers (1/28)<br>• K-1 teachers' Assessment data to Schmidt ASAP (1/21) |
| 01/13/05 | 7, 8 | | • Collaborative scoring began and rubric for comprehension was reviewed; Teachers are staying after school to continue scoring. | • Teachers' scoring completed and data submitted (1/21) |
| 01/19/05 | K, 1 | | • Upcoming Mini-Courses from Project Read<br>• 1st grade in on Assessments; Literacy Coach gave us the professional development schedule<br>• Literacy Coach and one teacher will grade assessments.<br>• There are no more "anchor papers" for Fluency. | |
| 01/19/05 | 4, 5, 6 | | • "I can" statements were edited for grade-level outcomes in the binders; Formal "I cans" were completed for fourth grade in all components.<br>• Reminder about scoring Thursday 3:00–5:00 p.m; All data due on 1/21. | • Teachers' assessment data submitted (1/21) |

*Chapter 5* (cont.)

**Appendix 5.1 Sample Grade-Level Team Minutes School Year 2005** *(cont.)*

| Date | Grade Levels | Agenda Item(s) | Discussion | Actions to be completed |
|---|---|---|---|---|
| 01/19/05 | 7, 8 | | • "I can" statements were reviewed for grade-level outcomes.<br>• Curriculum guide work was discussed. | • Teachers' assessment data submitted (1/21) |
| 01/20/05 | K, 1 | | • Do Gallery Walk preparation during grade-level meeting on 1/27.<br>• Assessment/Portfolio work | |
| 01/26/05 | 4, 5, 6 | | • Gallery Walk presentations were reviewed.<br>• Curriculum Guides were reviewed and graphs were distributed. | • Teachers Gallery Walk and Curriculum Guide Review (1/28)<br>• Administrative Decision: Can we get an extension on the Monday deadline for student lists for support services? Currently we have lesson plans, report cards, remediation plans, binders, and Gallery Walk due. |
| 01/26/05 | 7, 8 | | • Gallery Walk presentations were reviewed.<br>• Curriculum Guides were reviewed and graphs were distributed. | |
| 01/27/05 | K, 1 | | • Review of Gallery Walk, presentations, etc.<br>• Curriculum Binders may be arranged in the most appropriate way for us; Binders will be reviewed using a rubric tomorrow. | Literacy Coach:<br>• K-Fluency procedures to Kinder teachers (1/28) |
| 02/02/05 | K, 1 | Curriculum Guides | • See where people are: What's working? What's not working?<br>• Outcomes: 1) Pacing Chart/Rubric by quarter; 2) Strategies—Set up a Share Binder | |

*Chapter 5* (cont.)

**Appendix 5.2  School Professional Development Plans, School Year 2005**

| Date | Topic/Event | Evidence/Focus | Document Type | Additional Info |
|------|-------------|----------------|---------------|-----------------|
| 08/30/04 | SY05 Professional Development Plan | • Overview of PD for the school year | • PD Plan | • PD Plan |
| 09/20/04 | Revised Timelines for Lesson Plans, Due Dates, and Assessment Scoring | Change in due date for quarterly lesson plans since teachers are still scoring assessments.  Revised plan:<br>• 09/22: score writing and math assessments<br>• 09/23: score comprehension; curriculum planning<br>• 09–28: analyze scored assessments; determine key benchmarks to address based on data | • Memo from Literacy Coaches | |
| 09/28/04 | Curriculum Guide and Grade-Level Curriculum Work | • Curriculum Guide: introduction; sample viewing; questions.<br>• Grade-Level Curriculum Work: review/ edit outcomes and skills; insert "I Can" statements; discuss/analyze assessments | • Agenda: Restructured Day, 12:50– 2:30 p.m. | |
| 11/02/04 | Gallery Walk | • South Loop teachers presented assessment data and mini–lessons designed to address student learning needs.  The day ended with collaborative curriculum planning. | • Agenda: 8:30 a.m.–2:20 p.m. | |
| 11/19/04 | Assessments Mini–Course: 1–3:30 p.m. | • UIC professor | • November PD Plan | |
| 01/28/05 | Gallery Walk | • Teachers display, review, and provide comments on grade-level curriculum. Teachers present assessment data to colleagues.  Teachers submitted curriculum binders for review. | • Agenda 8:30 a.m.–2:45 p.m. | • Teacher notes on the Gallery Walk: questions, suggestions, thoughts, comments; Curriculum rubric guide and results |

**Appendix 5.2  School Professional Development Plans, 2005** *(cont.)*

| Date | Topic/Event | Evidence/Focus | Document Type | Additional Info |
|------|-------------|----------------|---------------|-----------------|
| 01/28/05 | Curriculum Guide | • Four categories in the rubric to guide the work: Goals for Student Learning; Instructional Plan; Instructional Strategies and Materials; Assessments (beginning, middle, and end of the year): comprehension, writing, fluency, math extended response | • Curriculum Guide Rubric: Teachers submitted curriculum binders to school administration for review and evaluation for completeness | • Evidence of teacher feedback for some teachers |
| 01/28/05 | Gallery Walk Feedback | • Teachers provide written feedback for colleagues based on the following categories: questions, suggestions, thoughts, or comments. | • Gallery Walk Feedback Form | • Teacher feedback for colleagues |
| 01/31/05 | Gallery Walk Results | • Review of agenda for the day; Descriptive feedback from administration to teachers: Positive Outcomes; Challenges; Administrative Follow–Up | • Qualitative Summary of 01/28/05 Gallery Walk | • 1-page document |
| 05/14/05 | Assessments and Curriculum | • Session 1: Collaboratively score assessments; Session 2: Modify end–of–year assessments (comprehension, writing, math); Session 3:Work on Curriculum Guides | • Schedule for Saturday 5/14/05 | |
| 05/27/05 | Gallery Walk | • Teachers display, review, and provide comments on grade-level curriculum; Teachers present assessment data to colleagues. | • PD Plan | |

*Chapter 6*

## Appendix 6.1. SLES and District Reflective Dialogue Survey Results, 2003. Percent of Teachers Endorsing Each Statement.

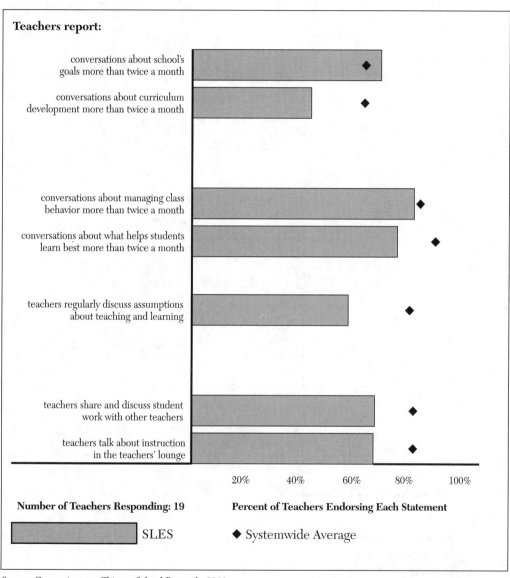

Source: Consortium on Chicago School Research, 2003.

*Chapter 6 (cont.)*

## Appendix 6.2. SLES and District Reflective Dialogue Survey Results, 2007.

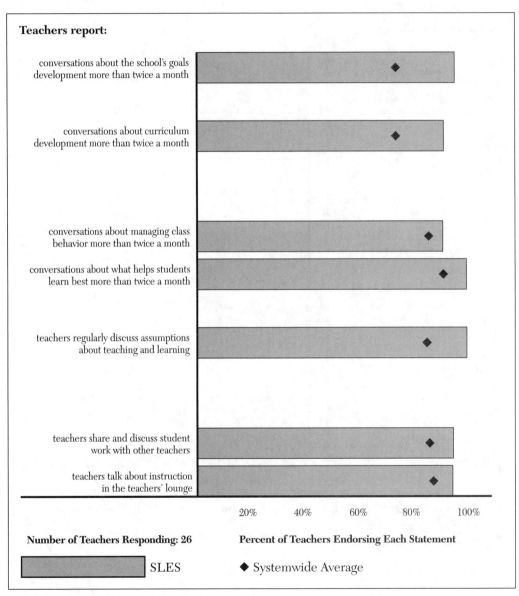

Source: Consortium on Chicago School Research, 2007.

*Chapter 6* (cont.)

## Appendix 6.3. SLES and District Collective Responsibility Survey Results, 2003. Percent of Teachers Endorsing Each Statement.

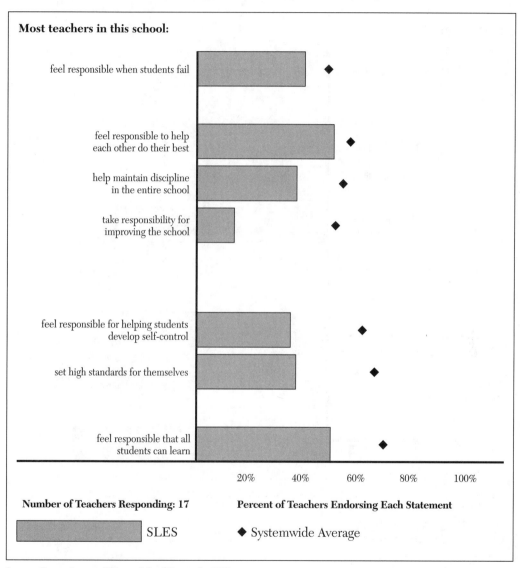

Source: Consortium on Chicago School Research, 2003.

*Chapter 6 (cont.)*

**Appendix 6.4. SLES and District Collective Responsibility Survey Results, 2007. Percent of Teachers Endorsing Each Statement.**

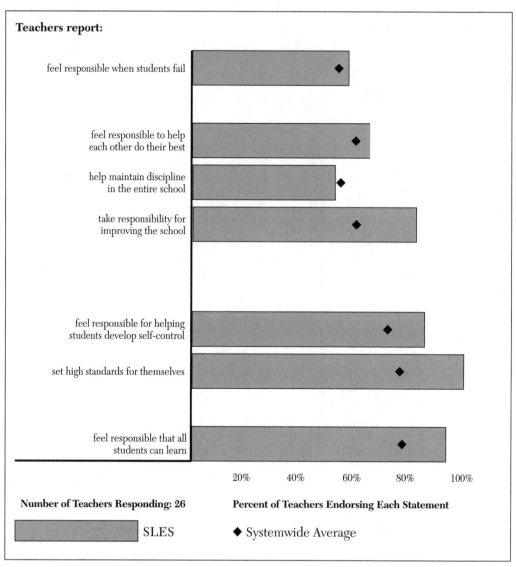

Source: Consortium on Chicago School Research, 2007.

*Chapter 6 (cont.)*

## Appendix 6.5. SLES and District Innovation Survey Results, 2003.
## Percent of Teachers Endorsing Each Statement.

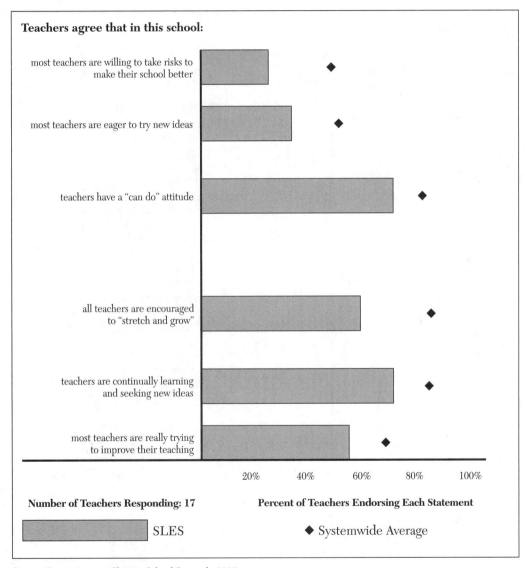

**Teachers agree that in this school:**

most teachers are willing to take risks to
make their school better

most teachers are eager to try new ideas

teachers have a "can do" attitude

all teachers are encouraged
to "stretch and grow"

teachers are continually learning
and seeking new ideas

most teachers are really trying
to improve their teaching

20%  40%  60%  80%  100%

**Number of Teachers Responding: 17**   **Percent of Teachers Endorsing Each Statement**

SLES    ◆ Systemwide Average

Source: Consortium on Chicago School Research, 2003.

*Chapter 6 (cont.)*

## Appendix 6.6.  SLES and District Innovation Survey Results, 2007. Percent of Teachers Endorsing Each Statement.

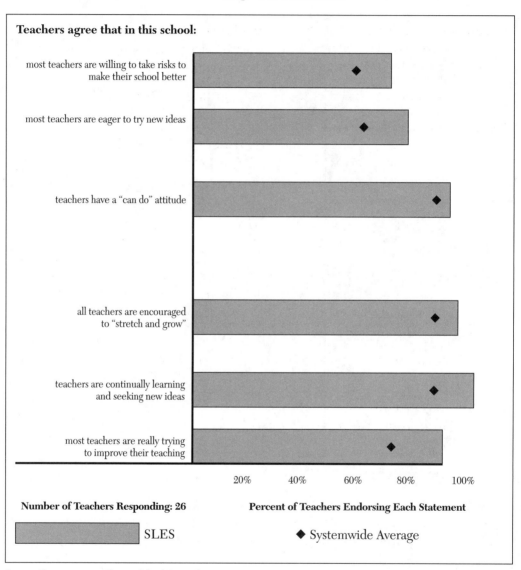

**Teachers agree that in this school:**

most teachers are willing to take risks to make their school better

most teachers are eager to try new ideas

teachers have a "can do" attitude

all teachers are encouraged to "stretch and grow"

teachers are continually learning and seeking new ideas

most teachers are really trying to improve their teaching

20%    40%    60%    80%    100%

**Number of Teachers Responding: 26**        **Percent of Teachers Endorsing Each Statement**

SLES        ◆ Systemwide Average

Source: Consortium on Chicago School Research, 2007.

# References Cited

Amrein, A. L. and D. C. Berliner. 2002. High-stakes testing, uncertainty, and student learning. *Education Policy Analysis Archives* 10 (18). http://epaa.asu.edu/epaa/v10n18/.

———. 2003. The effects of high-stakes testing on student motivation and learning. *Educational Leadership* 60 (5): 32–38.

Au, K. H. and S. Y. Hirata. 2005. Negotiating the slippery slope: School change and literacy achievement. *Journal of Literacy Research* 37 (3).

Au, K. H., S. Y. Hirata, and T. E. Raphael. 2005. Inspiring literacy achievement through standards. *The California Reader* 39 (1): 5–11.

Baccellieri, P. H. 2009. Using standardized and formative assessment to influence change in an urban school. Ph.D. diss., University of Illinois at Chicago.

Banchero, S. Despite fast strides, some still fall short. *The Chicago Tribune*, section 2, p. 1, section 2, p. 8. November 9, 2005. http://www.chicagotribune.com

Barth, R. 2006. Improving relationships within the schoolhouse. *Educational Leadership* 63 (6): 8–13.

Bernhardt, V. L. 2003. No schools left behind. *Educational Leadership* 60 (5): 26–30.

Black, P., C. Harrison, C. Lee, B. Marshall, and D. Wiliam. 2004. Working inside the black box: Assessment for learning in the classroom. *Phi Delta Kappan* 86 (1): 9–21.

Boudett, K. P., E. A. City, and R. J. Murnane. 2005. *Data Wise.* Cambridge, MA: Harvard Education Press.

———2006. The "data wise" improvement process: Eight steps for using test data to improve teaching and learning. *Harvard Education Letter* 22 (1): 1–3.

Buhle, R., and C. L. Z. Blachowicz. 2009. The assessment double play. *Educational Leadership* 66 (4): 42–46.

Chicago Tribune Editorial Board. Five more great ideas for the classroom. The fifth in a series: From here to excellence. The *Chicago Tribune*, February 7, 2007. http://www.chicagotribune.com

Cohen, D., and H. Hill. 2001. *Learning policy.* New Haven, CT: Yale University Press.

Consortium on Chicago School Research (CCSR). 2003. Individual school survey report.

Consortium on Chicago School Research (CCSR). 2007. Individual school survey report.

Consortium on Chicago School Research (CCSR). n.d. *South Loop School Individual School Page, Demographics.* http://www.consortium-chicago.org/Va2/Reports/Sch/3960/demog.tab

Consortium on Chicago School Research (CCSR). n.d. *South Loop School Individual School Page, 1990–1997 ITBS Results.* http://www.consortium-chicago.org/Va2/Reports/Sch/3960/itbs.tab

Crow, T. 2008. Declaration of interdependence: Q&A with Judith Warren Little. *Journal of Staff Development* 29 (3): 53–56.

Darling-Hammond, L. 2003. Keeping good teachers: Why it matters what teachers can do. *Educational Leadership* 60 (8): 6–13.

David, J. L. 2009. Collaborative inquiry. *Educational Leadership* 66 (4): 87–88.

Doyle, D. P. 2002. Knowledge-based decision making. *The School Administrator* 59 (11): 30–34.

DuFour, R. 2004. What is a "professional learning community"? *Educational Leadership* 61 (8): 6–11.

DuFour, R., and R. Eaker. 1998. *Professional learning communities at work: Best practices for enhancing student achievement.* Bloomington, IN: National Educational Service.

Dutro, E., M. Fisk, R. Koch, L. Roop, and K. Wixson. 2002. When state policies meet local district contexts: Standards-based professional development as a means to individual agency and collective ownership. *Teachers College Record* 104 (4): 787–811.

Eaker, R., and J. Keating. 2008. Collective commitments focus on change that benefits student learning. *Journal of Staff Development* 29 (3): 14–17.

Earl, L., and S. Katz. 2000. Changing classroom assessment: Teachers' struggles. In *The sharp edge of educational change: Teaching, leading and the realities of reform*, ed. N Bascia and A. Hargreaves, 97–111. London: Falmer Press.

Elmore, R. F. 2000. *Building a new structure for school leadership.* Washington, DC: The Albert Shanker Institute. http://www.shankerinstitute.org/Downloades/building.pdf

———. 2002. *Bridging the gap between standards and achievement.* Washington, DC: The Albert Shanker Institute. http://www.shankerinstitute.org/Downloads/Bridging_Gap.pdf

Elmore, R., P. Peterson, and S. McCarthey. 1996. *Restructuring in the classroom: Teaching, learning and school organization.* San Francisco: Jossey-Bass.

Falk, B. 2000. *Using standards and assessment to learn.* Portsmouth, NH: Heinemann.

———. 2002. Standards-based reforms: Problems and possibilities. *Phi Delta Kappan* 93 (8): 612–20.

Fullan, M. 2005. *Leadership & sustainability: System thinkers in action.* Thousand Oaks, CA: Corwin Press.

Fullan, M., P. Hill, and C. Crévola. 2006. *Breakthrough.* Thousand Oaks, CA: Corwin Press.

Garmston, R., and B. Wellman. 1998. Teacher talk that makes a difference. *Educational Leadership* 55 (7): 30–34.

Ghandi, I. n.d. Cited in Quotes about literacy leadership and change. *Quote Collections from Choice Literacy.* http://www.choiceliteracy.com

Gibson, L. 2002a. April 4. A sinking ship. *Chicago Journal*, 1, 8. http://chicagojournal.com

Gibson, L. 2002b, April 4. In shambles. *Chicago Journal*, 7. http://chicagojournal.com

Gibson, L. 2002c, July 25. Need for speed in principal search. *Chicago Journal*, 1. http://chicagojournal.com

Giles, C., and A. Hargreaves. 2006. The sustainability of innovative schools as learning organizations and professional learning communities during standardized reform. *Educational Administration Quarterly* 42 (1): 124–56.

Grossman, P., and S. Wineberg. 2000. *What makes teacher community different from a gathering of teachers?* (paper). University of Washington: Center for the Study of Teaching and Policy. http://depts.washington.edu/ctpmail/PDFs/Community-GWW-01-2001-pdf

Haycock, K. 2005, June 8. Improving academic achievement and closing gaps between groups in the middle grades. Presentation at CASE Middle Level Summit. http://www.edtrust.org

Heritage, M. 2007. Formative assessment: What do teachers need to know and do? *Phi Delta Kappan* 89 (2): 140–45.

Hess, F. M. 2009. The new stupid. *Educational Leadership* 66 (4): 12–17.

Hopkins, D., and D. Reynolds. 2001. The past, present, and future of school improvement: Towards the third age. *British Educational Research Journal* 27 (4): 359–475.

Hord, S. M. 1997. *Professional learning communities: Communities of continuous inquiry and improvement.* Austin, TX: Southwest Educational Development Laboratory.

Hubbard, L., H. Mehan, and M. Stein. 2006. *Reforming as learning: School reform, organizational culture, and community politics in San Diego.* New York: Routledge.

Huffman, J., and A. Jacobsen. 2003. Perceptions of professional learning communities. *International Journal of Leadership in Education* 6 (3): 239–50.

Illinois State Board of Education. *South Loop Elementary School 2006 Illinois School Report Card.* http://webprod.isbe.net/ereportcard/publicsite/searchBySchool.aspx?searchby=schoolName&language=english&year=2006&keyword=south%20loop&type=card

Joyce, B., and B. Showers. 2002. *Student achievement through staff development.* 3rd ed. Alexandria, VA: Association for Supervision and Curriculum Development.

Langer, G. M., A. B. Colton, and L. S. Goff. 2003. *Collaborative analysis of student work: Improving teaching and learning.* Alexandria, VA: Association for Supervision and Curriculum Development.

Lewin, K. n.d. Cited in Change quote collection. *Quote Collections from Choice Literacy.* http://www.choiceliteracy.com

Lieberman, A., and L. Miller. 2008. *Teachers in professional communities: Improving teaching and learning.* New York: Teachers College Press.

Maidenberg, M. 2008. Cloning South Loop School: Putting best educational practices "in a box." *Chicago Journal* 1 (October 29). http://chicagojournal.com

McLaughlin, M., and J. Talbert. 2003 (September). *Reforming districts: How districts support school reform.* A research report. Center for the Study of Teaching and Policy, University of Washington.

Morrison, J. 2008/2009. Why teachers must be data experts. *Educational Leadership* 66 (4). Online article at: http://www.ascd.org/publications/education_leadership/dec08/vol66

National Center for Education Statistics. 2000, August. *NAEP 1999 Trends in Academic Progress: Three Decades of Student Performance*, NCES 2000-469, by J.R. Campbell, C.M. Hombo, and J. Mazzeo. Washington, DC. http://nces.ed.gov/nationsreportcard//pubs/main1999/20000469.asp. It said "cannot download requested information."

National Center for Education Statistics. n.d. *The nation's report card: State reading 2003, Illinois grade 4 public schools.* Washington, DC. http://nces.ed.gov/nationsreportcard/pdf/stt2003/2004456IL4.pdf

National Center for Education Statistics. n.d. *The nation's report card: State reading 2003, Illinois grade 8 public schools.* Washington, DC. http://nces.ed.gov/nationsreportcard/pdf/stt2003/2004456IL8.pdf

National Center for Education Statistics. n.d. *Reading: The NAEP reading achievement levels.* Washington, DC. http://nces.ed.gov/nationsreportcard/reading/achieveall.asp

National Center for Education Statistics. n.d. *Reading: The status of achievement levels.* Washington, DC. http://nces.ed.gov/nationsreportcard/achlevdev.asp?id=rd

National Center for Education Statistics. n.d. *State profiles: Achievement levels for reading, national public.* Washington, DC. http://nces.ed.gov/nationsreportcard/states/achievement.asp

National Center for Education Statistics. n.d. *Trial Urban District Assessment Snapshot Reports*. Washington, DC. http://nces.ed.gov/nationsreportcard/reading/results2003/districtsnapshot.asp

Payne, C. 2002. So much reform, so little change. In *Education Policy for the 21st Century: Challenges and Opportunities in Standards-Based Reform*, ed. L. B. Joseph, 239–78. Champaign, IL: University of Illinois Press.

Pollard, W. n.d. Cited in *Thinkexist.com*. http://en.thinkexist.com/quotes/william_pollard/

Porter, J. n.d. Cited in *Change quote collection*. Choice Literacy. http://www.choiceliteracy.com

Raphael, T. E., K. H. Au, and S. R. Goldman. (in press). Whole school instructional improvement through the Standards-Based Change Process: A developmental model. In J. Hoffman and Y. Goodman (eds.) *Changing Literacies for Changing Times*. New York: Routledge/Taylor & Francis Group.

Richardson, J. 2002. Take a closer look. *Tools for Schools* 5 (5): 1–2.

Routman, R. 2002. Teacher talk. *Educational Leadership* 59 (6): 32–35.

Sarason, S. 1990. *The predictable failure of educational reform: Can we change course before it's too late*. San Francisco: Jossey Bass.

———. 1995. *School change: The personal development of a point of view*. New York: Teachers College Press.

Schlechty, P. 1997. *Inventing better schools: An action plan for educational reform*. San Francisco: Jossey Bass.

Schmoker, M. 2004. Tipping point: From feckless reform to substantive instructional improvement. *Phi Delta Kappan* 85 (6): 424–32.

————. 2006. *Results now: How we can achieve unprecedented improvements in teaching and learning.* Alexandria, VA: Association for Supervision and Curriculum Development.

Sebring, P., E. Allensworth, A. Bryk, J. Easton, and S. Luppescu. 2006 (September). The essential supports for school improvement. The Consortium on Chicago School Research CCSR) at the University of Chicago, Research Report. http://ccsr.uchicago.edu/publications/EssentialSupports.pdf

Sharkey, N. S., and R. J. Murnane. 2003. Learning from student assessment results. *Educational Leadership* 61 (3): 77–81.

————. 2006. Tough choices in designing a formative assessment system. *American Journal of Education* 112 (4): 572–88.

Stafford, K. n.d. Cited in *Favorite mentoring quotes.* Choice Literacy. http://www.choiceliteracy.com

State Board of Education eReport Card Public Site. http://webprod.isbe.net/ereportcard/publicsite/getReport.aspx?year=2005$code=150162990_e.pdf.

Stiggins, R. 2004. New assessment beliefs for a new school mission. *Phi Delta Kappan* 86 (1): 22–27.

Tanner, J. Born of controversy, S. Loop School to open, *The Chicago Tribune*, sec. 2, February 15, 1988. http://www.chicagotribune.com

Taylor, B., M. Pearson, K. Clark, and S. Walpole. 2000. Effective schools and accomplished teachers: Primary-grade reading instruction in low-income Schools. *The Elementary School Journal* 101 (2): 121–65.

Taylor, B., M. Peterson, P. D. Pearson, and M. C. Rodriguez. 2002. Looking inside classrooms: Reflecting on the "how" as well as the "what" in effective reading instruction. *The Reading Teacher* 56 (3): 270–79.

———. 2005. The CIERA School Change Framework: An evidence-based approach to professional development and school reading improvement. *Reading Research Quarterly* 40 (1): 40–69.

Taylor, B. M., T. E. Raphael, and K. H. Au. (in press). School reform in reading. In P. D. Pearson, M. Kamil, P. Afflerback, and E. Dutrow (eds.), *Handbook of Reading Research*. New York: Routledge/Taylor & Francis Group.

Von Frank, V. 2008. The gift of time. *The Learning Principal* 4 (3): 1, 6–7.

Wagner, T., R. Kegan, L. Lahey, R. Lemons, J. Garnier, D. Helsing, A. Howell, and H. Rasmussen. 2006. *Change leadership: A practical guide to transforming our schools*. San Francisco: Jossey-Bass.

Wayman, J. C., and S. Stringfield. 2006. Technology-supported involvement of entire faculties in examination of student data for instructional improvement. *American Journal of Education* 112 (4): 549–71.

Weissmann, D. 1997. Bridging the class chasm in South Loop. *Catalyst Chicago* 9 (3). http://www.catalyst-chicago.org/11-97/117chasm.htm

Yin, R. 2003. *Case Study Research: Design and Methods*. Thousand Oaks, CA: Sage Publications, Inc.

Young, V. M. 2006. Teachers' use of data: Loose coupling, agenda setting, and team norms. *American Journal of Education* 112 (4): 521–48.